HOLY FUCK
WE ARE ALL GOING TO...
A) HELL
B) PRISON
C) BOTH
BUT IT'S WORTH IT, BELIEVE ME.
IF I ABSOLUTELY HAVE TO GO TO JAIL FOR A COMIC-BOOK MOVIE THEN I ACCEPT NO SUBSTITUTES.
THIS IS THE ONE.
— MARK MILLAR
ON HIS FIRST VISIT TO THE SET
D0470705

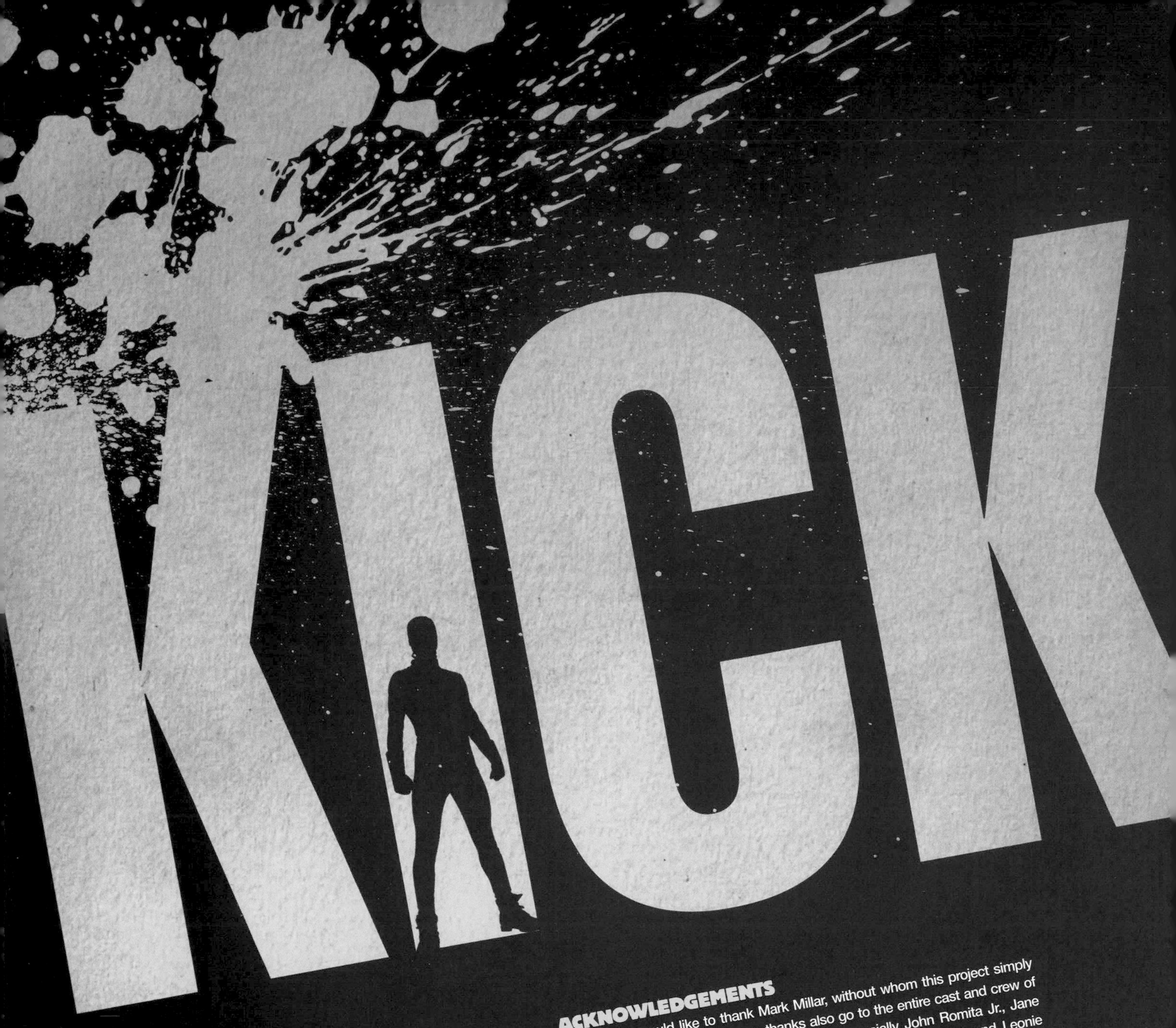

KICK-ASS: CREATING THE COMIC MAKING THE MOVIE

ISBN 9781848564091

Published by
Titan Books
A division of
Titan Publishing Group Ltd
144 Southwark St
London
SE1 0UP

First edition February 2010
1 2 3 4 5 6 7 8 9 10

Book design by Martin Stiff.

ACKNOWLEDGEMENTS

Titan Books would like to thank Mark Millar, without whom this project simply would not have happened. Huge thanks also go to the entire cast and crew of *Kick-Ass* for their enthusiastic co-operation, especially John Romita Jr., Jane Goldman and Matthew Vaughn. We're indebted to Tarquin Pack and Leonie Mansfield at KA Productions for making the process of putting this book together so smooth. Many thanks to unit publicist Stacy Mann and Jeremy Smith (AKA Mr Beaks) for their help, and especially to Mark Salisbury for his incisive extended interviews with Mark Millar, John Romita Jr. and Jane Goldman.

Visit our website: **www.titanbooks.com**

Did you enjoy this book? We love to hear from our readers. Please e-mail us at: **readerfeedback@titanemail.com** or write to Reader Feedback at the above address.

A CIP catalogue record for this title is available from the British Library.

Printed and bound in the USA.

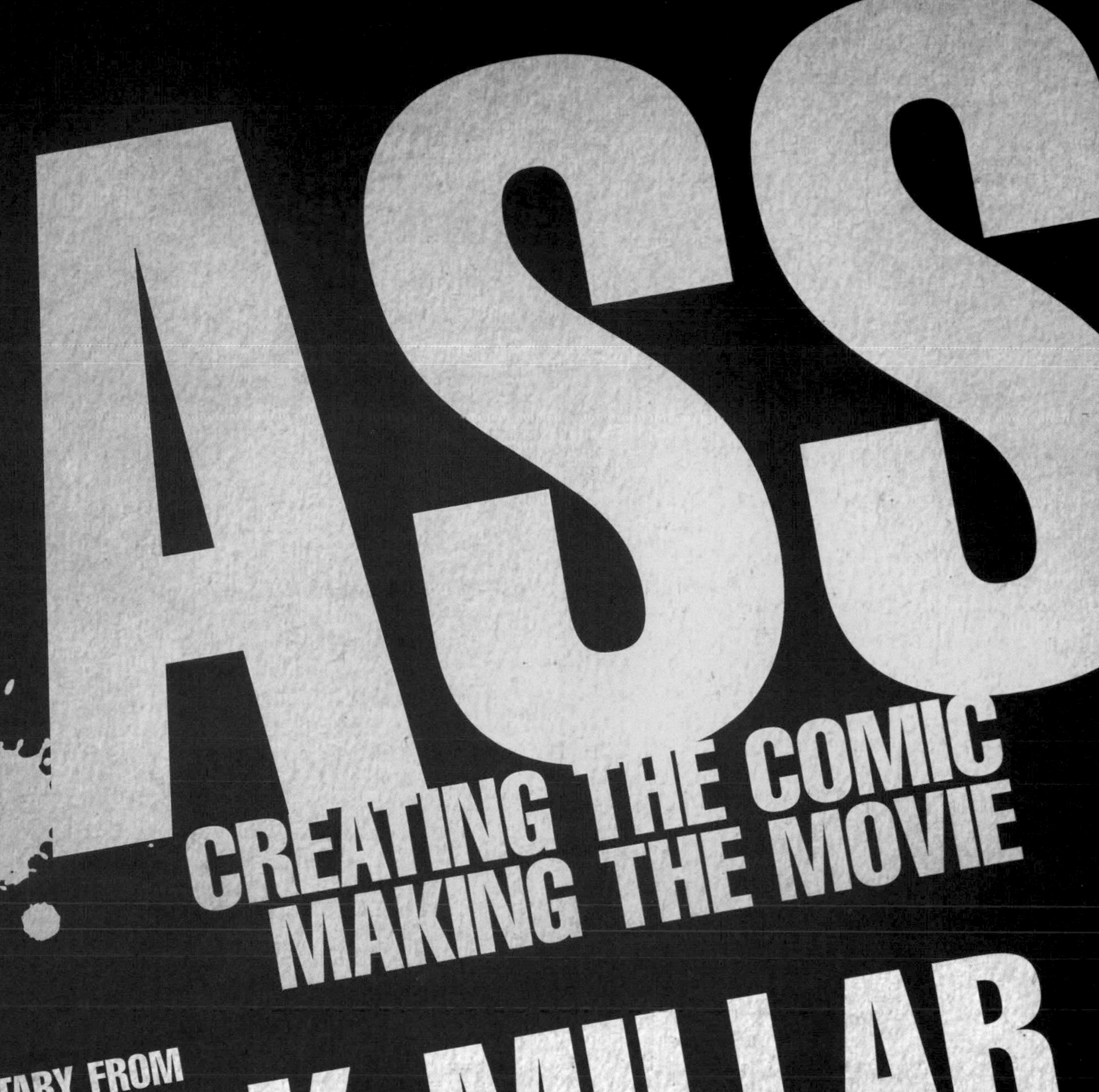

CREATING THE COMIC
MAKING THE MOVIE

COMMENTARY FROM
MARK MILLAR
WITH CONTRIBUTIONS FROM MEMBERS OF THE CAST AND CREW

INTERVIEWS BY MARK SALISBURY
STACY MANN AND JEREMY SMITH

FEATURING EXCERPTS FROM THE SCREENPLAY BY
JANE GOLDMAN & MATTHEW VAUGHN

KICK-ASS CREATED BY
MARK MILLAR AND JOHN ROMITA JR.

TITAN BOOKS

CONTENTS

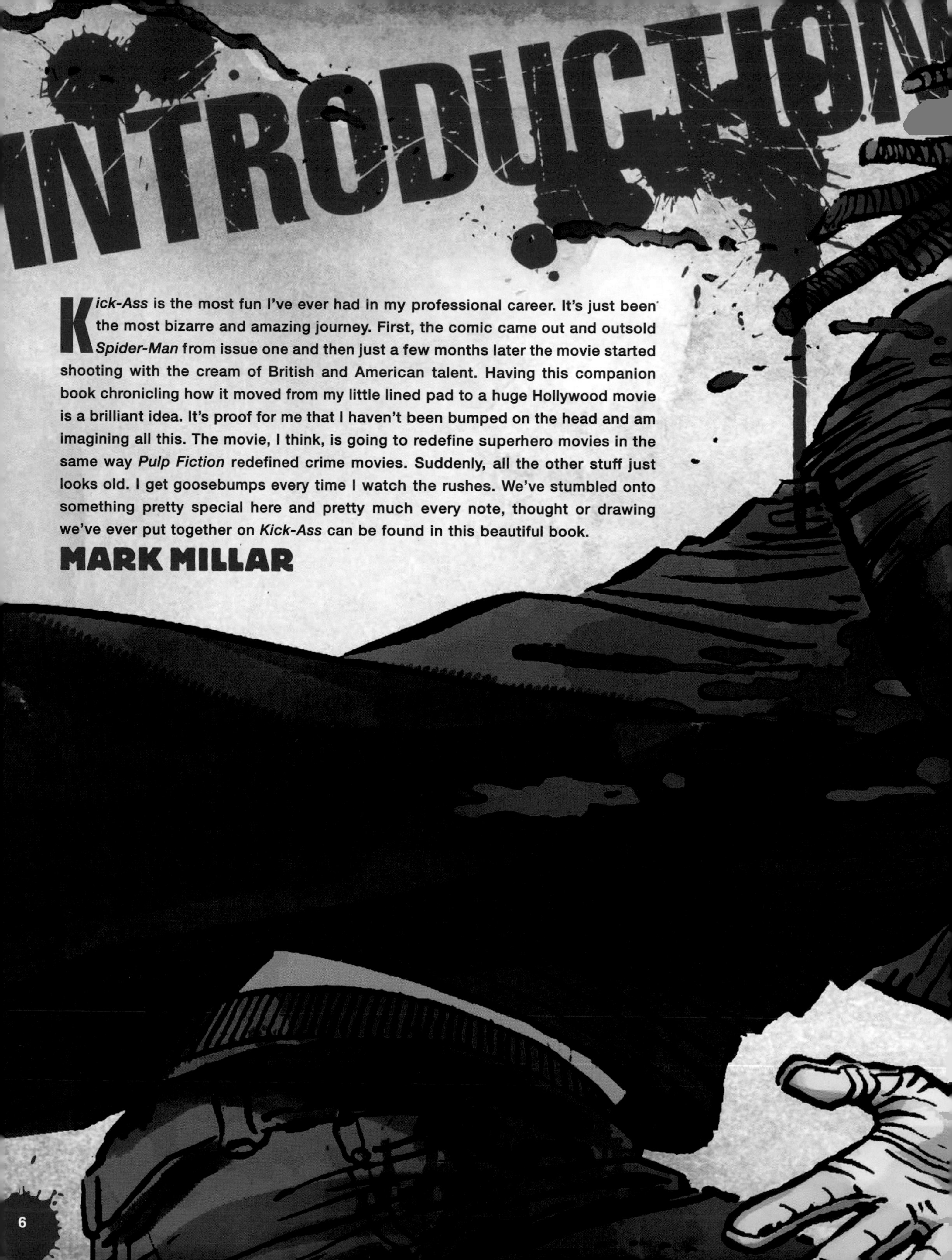

INTRODUCTION

Kick-Ass is the most fun I've ever had in my professional career. It's just been the most bizarre and amazing journey. First, the comic came out and outsold *Spider-Man* from issue one and then just a few months later the movie started shooting with the cream of British and American talent. Having this companion book chronicling how it moved from my little lined pad to a huge Hollywood movie is a brilliant idea. It's proof for me that I haven't been bumped on the head and am imagining all this. The movie, I think, is going to redefine superhero movies in the same way *Pulp Fiction* redefined crime movies. Suddenly, all the other stuff just looks old. I get goosebumps every time I watch the rushes. We've stumbled onto something pretty special here and pretty much every note, thought or drawing we've ever put together on *Kick-Ass* can be found in this beautiful book.

MARK MILLAR

But perhaps I'm getting ahead of myself. Perhaps it's wise to just start at the beginning...

KICK-ASS

is all about a wee guy in the real world, our world, who doesn't have powers from the planet Krypton, he hasn't been bitten by a radioactive spider, he doesn't have all the trappings of a comic book superhero, he's just a guy like you or me who decides that his life is so dull, with school and television and DVD box sets and computer games, that he wants to live the life of a superhero.

On the one hand he's doing it because he's bored, but on the other hand he genuinely wants to make a difference. He's read enough superhero comics that for him the greatest thing he could do is go out and help his fellow man, so it's kind of lovely in a weird way. It's oddly charming as well as being disgustingly violent.

Kick-Ass is my love letter to superhero comics, and I've taken little parts of my own life and the lives of friends and shoved it all in there to make the characters as real as possible.

I think Kick-Ass is a superhero people can identify with, because as much as Peter Parker's an everyman, he is still going out with Kirsten Dunst, climbing walls, swinging about on webs and fighting the Green Goblin. This is a guy in the real world, coming up against some real-life bad stuff when he tries to help folk.

It all started when I was about fifteen. My friend Paul (who I later dedicated the comic to) and I, we genuinely had a plan to become superheroes. Rather than being a teacher, a doctor, or a lawyer, we thought — seriously, it was a career option for us — "No, we want to be superheroes. This is what we want to do." Frank Miller's *Year One* was out at the time, Alan Moore was doing his realistic superhero stuff, and we were sitting in the lunchroom saying, "Why don't we do this?" We were really enjoying the comics! It sounds so corny but it's a hundred per cent true. We came up with names and we designed a costume each. We started karate, we were going to the gym, and we were *actually* going to do what Batman had done.

It's amazing how incredibly derivative our stuff was. My pal's superhero name was "Batman". I came up with a few different names. The one I remember most was Mr. Danger. He was a Rorschach-style character, because I didn't want to wear a skin-tight costume — I was going to wear a trench coat and a mask and a hat and everything.

We were at it for a year, we were going to the gym and lifting weights every day and getting ourselves quite pumped up. It's probably the fittest I've ever been in my life. We absolutely had a plan. And this was before the internet, so we didn't know if we were ever going to hook up with anyone else. It was just him and me.

We were going to patrol the area and take on organized crime. Now bear in mind I grew up in a small town in the west of Scotland, so there's no Martin Scorsese-style stuff going on — at worst you've got a few drunks hanging about, sheep rustling maybe — but our plan was to go out and just kick some ass. And we're both five foot eight and couldn't fight our way out of a paper bag; we would have been killed instantly, so thank God it never happened. We decided to get fat and stop exercising and read comics instead.

But the story has always been in my head; what would have happened if we hadn't come to our senses and decided not to do this? *Kick-Ass* is that story — what would happen next, if you put that costume on, went out, your first night on patrol?

Sc. 13 INT. DAVE'S KITCHEN — DAY.

29.

WHEN THAT LIGHTENING FLASH CLEARS, WE'RE BACK IN THE KITCHEN, PRESENT DAY. THE GRAVESTONE IS BACK BEING THE CERIAL BOX.
(STOP CAMERA MOVE.)

DAVE LOOKS AT THE BOX.

O.T.S. DAD TO DAVE.

ML: "THEY NEVER HAD SO MANY MALLOW..."

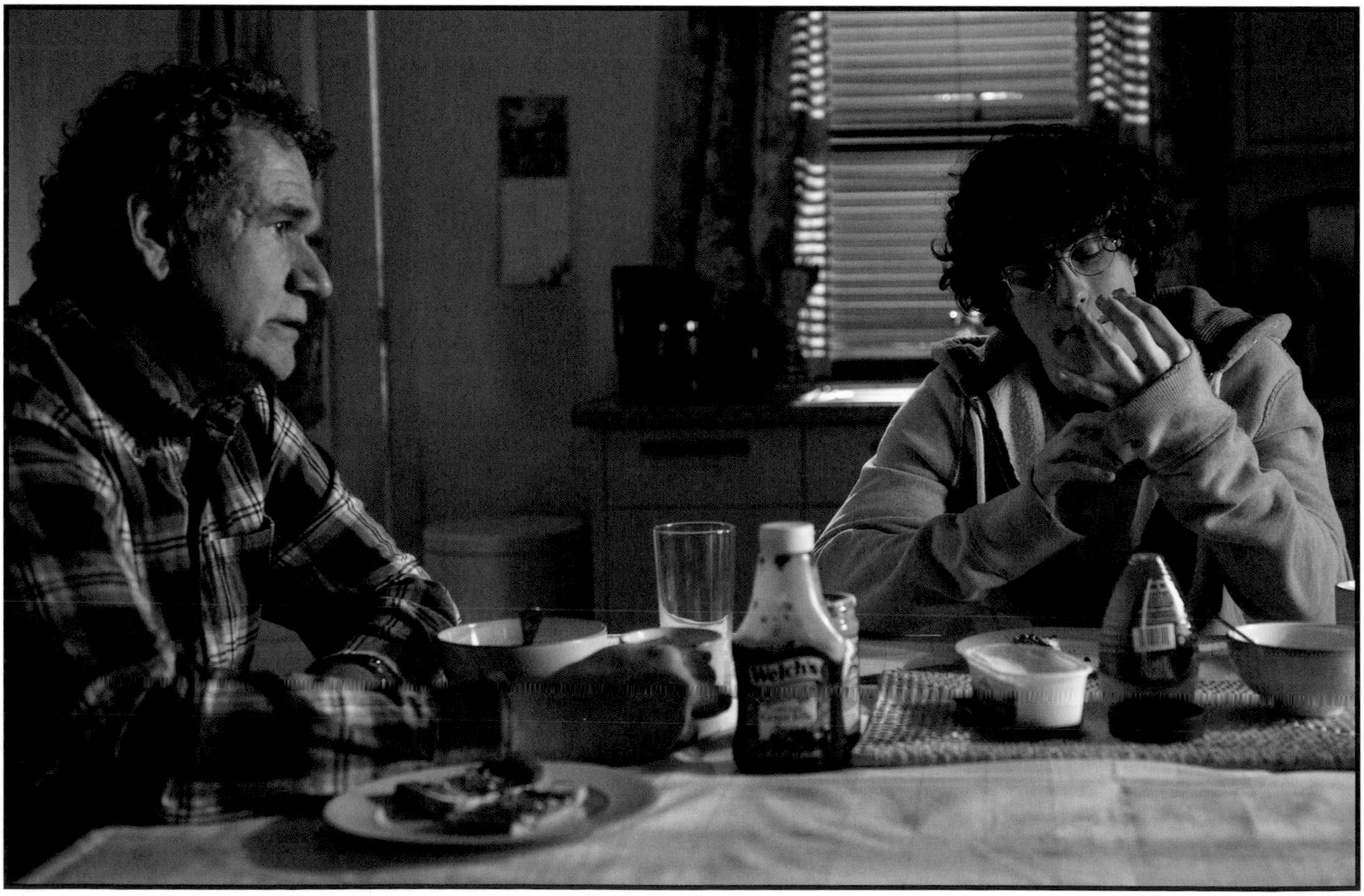

REVERSE — O.T.S. DAVE TO DAD.

It's funny because when I came to write the first issues of *Kick-Ass* I didn't realize how autobiographical it was. I just wanted to create a convincing character of that age, and because I was, at that age, as into comics as he is, it really wasn't that much of a leap for me. All I did was update things — so instead of hanging around the comic store talking about superheroes, these kids are on MySpace and the Newsarama forums, which is exactly what I'd have been doing if I'd been born twenty years later. But small things, like Dave pretends he's gay to get close to this girl he really likes, that's a slightly more outrageous version of something I did.

There was a girl I really fancied at school, and she used to sit beside me in some classes, so I'd see her about half of the week, and we got on really well, but I wasn't sure how easy it was going to be to ask her out. I wanted to get as many things in common with her as possible — I was very calculating. You know, the sort of stupid things you do when you're a teenager just to meet girls. She was really into *Dynasty* and *The Colbys*, bearing in mind this was 1985, so I went off and asked people who were into that stuff, "What's it all about?" watched the programs, got caught up with it, and became an expert on it within about three weeks. I got to go out with her based on a love of *Dynasty* and *The Colbys*, mine being entirely fictitious. I can still remember all these facts about *Dynasty* and *The Colbys* because of that. So I thought a funnier version would be that this girl's really politically correct, and she wants a Gay Best Friend to go shopping with, so Dave fakes being gay just to get close to her, hoping she'll fall in love with him. That's where all that came from.

EXT. GRAVE-YARD. NIGHT.

...A GRAVESTONE. Behind it, the New York skyline through a fierce storm. Dave: dripping wet, fists aloft, raging at the heavens through the thunder and lightning.

DAVE
I will avenge you, mother!

There's other stuff in there too. Dave lives alone with his dad, same as I did. When I was fourteen, my mum died, and I made Dave fourteen when his mum died as well. Some of it's sad, and some of it's funny, for example dad and I had the same meal for four years because it was all he could cook. He learned how to make mince and potatoes, and we had that every night, from when I was fourteen until I was eighteen. It's weird, I moaned about it, and I could have learned to cook myself, but I just couldn't be bothered. I just

MENTIN NAME BEING HIT-GIRL.
I GOT YOUR BACK.
NATT! COME BACK!
WE NEED TO TALK!
WE SUPERHEROES HAVE TO STICK TOGETHER, RIGHT?
what?
Running off.
No wait
WHO ARE YOU?
Come back a second
We need to talk
WE NEED TO TALK!
WHO ARE YOU PEOPLE?
WINK.
SLASH
SMACK
SMACK
SMACK
KILL
SMACK
KILL
KICK-ASS AND THE OTHER GUY ATTEND A FIRE.
GUY WINKS OVER TO HIM
COPS COMING AROUND.
HIGH-FIVE FOR DADDY.
what?
WINK.
GOES HOME + VOMITS THROUGH STEEL NERVES.
SHE WAS LIKE POCKET JOHN RAMBO
where are you going, cock-sucker?
Off to phone your bitch, liberal lawyer?
WELL, HILLARY AIN'T IN THE WHITE HOUSE YET, COCK-SUCKER
I CAN ONLY IMAGINE HOW THEY MUST HAVE FELT.
HIT-GIRL.

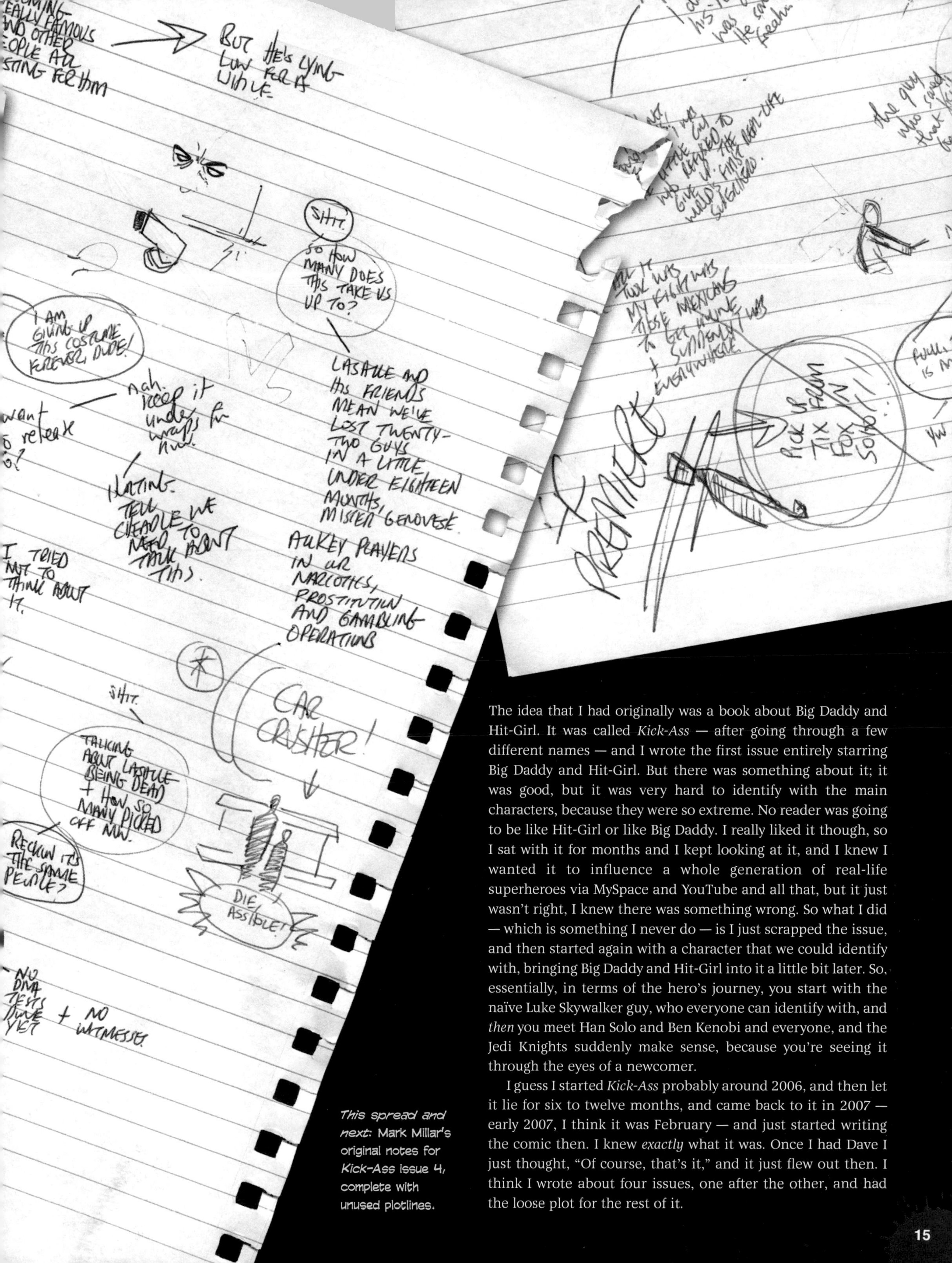

BUT HE'S LYING LOW FOR A WHILE
SHIT.
SO HOW MANY DOES THIS TAKE US UP TO?
I AM GIVING UP THIS COSTUME FOREVER, DUDE!
nah. keep it under wraps for now.
LASALLE AND HIS FRIENDS MEAN WE'VE LOST TWENTY-TWO GUYS IN A LITTLE UNDER EIGHTEEN MONTHS, MISTER GENOVESE.
I TRIED NOT TO THINK ABOUT IT.
PLAYERS IN OUR NARCOTICS, PROSTITUTION AND GAMBLING OPERATIONS
CAR CRUSHER!
SHIT.
TALKING ABOUT LASALLE BEING DEAD + HOW SO MANY PICKED OFF NOW.
RECKON IT'S THE SAME PEOPLE?
DIE, ASSHOLE!
NO DNA TESTS DONE YET + NO WITNESSES

The idea that I had originally was a book about Big Daddy and Hit-Girl. It was called *Kick-Ass* — after going through a few different names — and I wrote the first issue entirely starring Big Daddy and Hit-Girl. But there was something about it; it was good, but it was very hard to identify with the main characters, because they were so extreme. No reader was going to be like Hit-Girl or like Big Daddy. I really liked it though, so I sat with it for months and I kept looking at it, and I knew I wanted it to influence a whole generation of real-life superheroes via MySpace and YouTube and all that, but it just wasn't right, I knew there was something wrong. So what I did — which is something I never do — is I just scrapped the issue, and then started again with a character that we could identify with, bringing Big Daddy and Hit-Girl into it a little bit later. So, essentially, in terms of the hero's journey, you start with the naïve Luke Skywalker guy, who everyone can identify with, and *then* you meet Han Solo and Ben Kenobi and everyone, and the Jedi Knights suddenly make sense, because you're seeing it through the eyes of a newcomer.

I guess I started *Kick-Ass* probably around 2006, and then let it lie for six to twelve months, and came back to it in 2007 — early 2007, I think it was February — and just started writing the comic then. I knew *exactly* what it was. Once I had Dave I just thought, "Of course, that's it," and it just flew out then. I think I wrote about four issues, one after the other, and had the loose plot for the rest of it.

This spread and next: Mark Millar's original notes for *Kick-Ass* issue 4, complete with unused plotlines.

GANG BOSS SHOULD HAVE HIS BIG SCENE BEFORE THIS.
GIRLFRIEND ASSURES HIM SHE WON'T GO TO COPS, BUT WE'RE LEFT WITH A SILENT PANEL.
CUT TO RED MIST BECOMING A BIG THING AND OUR GUY JEALOUS.
THEN RED MIST GETS IN TOUCH AND THEY BECOME REALLY FRIENDLY.
THEN WE GET THE LITTLE MOMENT WITH BD + HG
THEN STUFF WITH THE FIRE + THEY REALLY BECOME FAMOUS AND INSPIRE OTHER HEROES.
BIG DADDY GETS IN TOUCH, BUT KICK-ASS DOESN'T WANT TO GET INVOLVED.
THEN GIRL GOES TO THE COPS AND CONFESSES ABOUT KICK-ASS.
KICK-ASS SHOULD BE INTERVIEWING OLD LADY + THE MISSING DOG.
GOES BACK HOME TO FIND DAD ARRESTED + COSTUME FOUND + COPS ... THEM AWAY.
HE'S DEVASTATED AND CAN'T TALK TO ANYONE ABOUT IT.
EVENTUALLY VISITS HIS DAD IN PRISON + SAD SCENE.
BIG SCENE WITH GIRL.
OSAMA BIN LADEN VS KICK-ASS
YOU TUBE SILLINESS!!

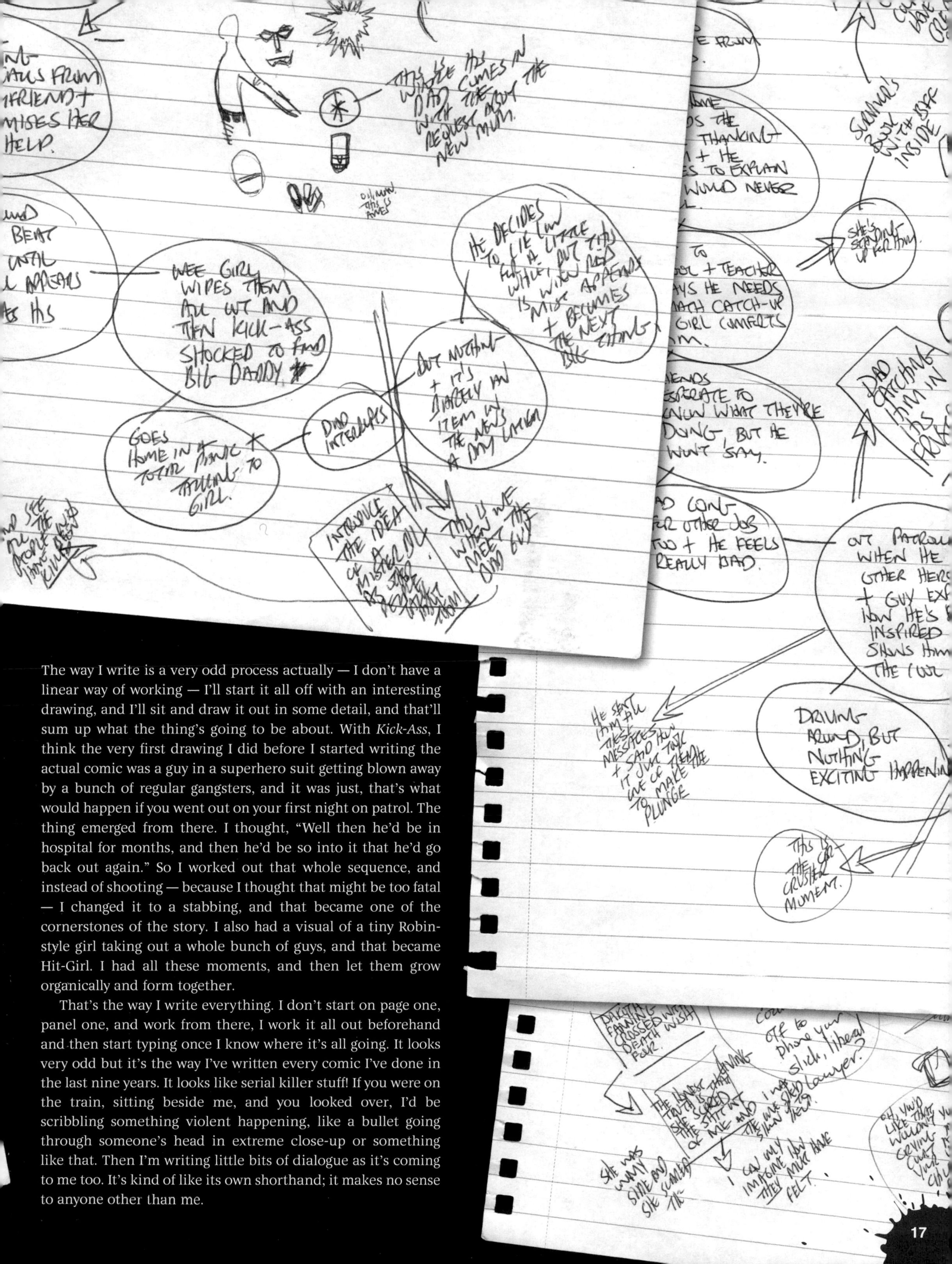

The way I write is a very odd process actually — I don't have a linear way of working — I'll start it all off with an interesting drawing, and I'll sit and draw it out in some detail, and that'll sum up what the thing's going to be about. With *Kick-Ass*, I think the very first drawing I did before I started writing the actual comic was a guy in a superhero suit getting blown away by a bunch of regular gangsters, and it was just, that's what would happen if you went out on your first night on patrol. The thing emerged from there. I thought, "Well then he'd be in hospital for months, and then he'd be so into it that he'd go back out again." So I worked out that whole sequence, and instead of shooting — because I thought that might be too fatal — I changed it to a stabbing, and that became one of the cornerstones of the story. I also had a visual of a tiny Robin-style girl taking out a whole bunch of guys, and that became Hit-Girl. I had all these moments, and then let them grow organically and form together.

That's the way I write everything. I don't start on page one, panel one, and work from there, I work it all out beforehand and then start typing once I know where it's all going. It looks very odd but it's the way I've written every comic I've done in the last nine years. It looks like serial killer stuff! If you were on the train, sitting beside me, and you looked over, I'd be scribbling something violent happening, like a bullet going through someone's head in extreme close-up or something like that. Then I'm writing little bits of dialogue as it's coming to me too. It's kind of like its own shorthand; it makes no sense to anyone other than me.

Subject: New Projects

Attachments: none

On 25 Oct 2007, at 12:53, **Mark Millar** wrote:

Hi Matthew,

Sorry to hear things didn't work out with Thor. I hope you get a chance to do the character at some point as your take sounded cool. Not sure what projects I have that would be interesting to you. I'm still doing 80% of my work at Marvel so don't really own a lot of it beyond Wanted, Chosen and The Unfunnies.

Have a couple of new things I'm writing at the moment, but neither is finished. The first is called Kick-Ass and nobody's seen anything yet, but it launches as a book at Marvel's creator-owned imprint in February. It's the idea of a wee guy in NYC just going out there in the real world and trying to be a superhero. I just started small and tried to think a) what you would do to start and b) the shit you could get into very quickly. It's done completely straight and quite unique. I've dropped hints online and in interviews about it, but the big marketing campaign I have planned is a cracker and I'll tell you about it once you've read these first two scripts. Also copied here is the ad/first issue cover, the copy simply reading 'FUCK CRIME'.

All the best,

MM

In late summer 2007, when I'd written the first four issues, I was introduced to Matthew Vaughn. I'd had a bit of a preconception about him before I met him, because he was part of that whole Guy Ritchie set, that '90s London Jack-the-Lad cockney gangster kind of thing, and I didn't think I would have anything in common with him at all. Then I read this interview with Matthew a couple of weeks before we actually got speaking on the phone, where he was talking about his favorite five movies of all time, and he put *The Incredibles* in there. I remember thinking, "I'm kind of surprised at that." It wasn't what I was expecting him to put. That was my first inkling that he would be a secret geek, and share the same passions that I do.

Then, when we got talking on the phone, we realized we had *everything* in common, and it was really odd, because he was born into this aristocratic family in the south of England, I was born into a working-class family in the west of Scotland. Our lives could not have seemed more different, but we actually agreed on almost everything. It was very odd that the first phone call we had — normally it's a five-minute, slightly strained phone call when you first meet somebody — I think we did two and a half hours, our first chat. Everything from *Jaws* to *Star Wars* to all that stuff in the '70s. We're about the same age, so everything hit us at exactly the right time. He's quite like me too, in that he has a love for the stuff but not this strangling loyalty that some writers have — like if I come up with an idea that contradicts *Justice League of America* issue 47 or something, that doesn't worry me too much if it's a good idea. Matthew's similarly ruthless. He loves *Spider-Man* and all that kind of stuff, but he's not beholden to the continuity, he didn't read the comics that much growing up, he was probably more into the movies and just the idea of it, the characters.

We've got quite a few mutual friends, and he invited me down to the *Stardust* premiere. He and I had talked on the phone about doing something together, but we didn't meet face to face until the party at his house after the *Stardust* premiere. That experience was actually pretty weird, but it was really cool. I went along with two friends, and literally everyone in the house was famous apart from us. My friend said to me — actually Bryan Hitch, the guy who draws *The Ultimates* — he said, "You're the only face here that I don't recognize!" because every single person Matthew knows happens to be a supermodel or a famous actor or whatever. It was quite surreal, it was kind of like the cover of the *Sergeant Pepper* album, just all these famous faces all crushed together, drinking at his free bar at his house. So we got talking then, and got on really well. We'd had several really long, two- or three-hour phone conversations beforehand, and it was one of those things where we just clicked.

Matthew and I decided we were going to do something together. We talked about two books. One of them was *Chosen*, which is now called *American Jesus*. We'd considered that, but the minute I sent him the scripts for *Kick-Ass*...

Above: John Romita Jr. (left) and Mark Millar, on the set of *Kick-Ass*.

MATTHEW VAUGHN READS THE SCRIPTS

Matthew fell in love with *Kick-Ass* when he read the first two scripts and said, "Can you send me the next one?" and I kept firing them down. I was writing the comic, and then *he* started writing the movie script when I was still writing the comic, and he overtook me. He knew the loose plot though, and where it was going. We met up and we talked about it and blocked the whole thing out, and it just happened so organically. At this point no agents had been involved, nothing. My agent was furious — "We could have shopped this, taken it around and got a good option going for it!" — especially as, by this point, the buzz on *Wanted* was big. He said we could have got a good deal. I was like, "Are you out of your mind? Nobody would make this film." Matthew's the only person that would have the balls to do something like this, really.

ENTER JOHN ROMITA JR.

Johnny and I had worked together on a project called *Wolverine: Enemy of the State*, and we really got on well personally. I love his stuff. I'd say he's one of my three favorite artists of all time, he's amazing. You don't really appreciate how good he is until you've worked with him and you see what he brings to a script, because he's got such a natural storytelling style. So we were keen to do something else together, that was the first factor. The other thing was, this had to be an urban, gritty style of comic, in the Frank Miller tradition, and if you did it with a standard American artist it wouldn't have worked. You needed somebody that would give it that Martin Scorsese, smoke-coming-out-of-the-manhole-covers feel, and nobody does that like Johnny. I couldn't have imagined anyone else drawing it — from the beginning it was just Johnny in my head. And as Johnny always does, it looks better than it was in my head.

Johnny's one of the best artists the industry's ever seen, and what he brought to *Kick-Ass* was that verisimilitude; it didn't look like a regular comic book, it looked like something a mainstream reader could pick up and understand.

Johnny's famous for being able to turn around a comic in record time, he's the fastest artist in the industry. Normally, a comic takes about five weeks, and Johnny has been known to do it in a weekend. He's a legend. It's always amazing, he knows exactly where to put the line. Actually, I think I'm the first person who's made him miss deadlines! Johnny famously never misses a deadline. He's got a career going back to 1977, and he never, *ever* misses a deadline, and I made him miss a deadline on this. *Kick-Ass* should have come out monthly, but he ended up getting so much work to do on it, not only from the amount I was asking for in comic scripts, but also he ended up doing lots of drawings to be used in the movie.

The minute we started talking on the phone and he was sending some sketches through, *Kick-Ass* suddenly began to crystallize, it seemed very, very exciting. I had a weird feeling that we were really onto something big here, and Johnny had the same feeling too. And we did have a lot of faith in the project originally, because we wrote it for free. We obviously got paid on the other side of it, but we really believed in the project so much that we wrote it for free and drew it for free and got no payment on it for a year so that we could own it one hundred per cent. We knew this was something worth owning, worth investing our time in.

Previous page, this spread and next: Romita's first design sketches for Kick-Ass's mask, Hit-Girl, Big Daddy, and Red Mist.

1ST SKETCHES OF BIG DADDY
1

2

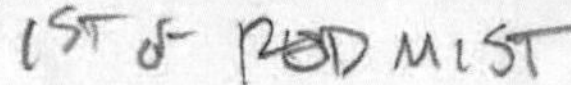

1

JOHN ROMITA JR. ON...

WORKING WITH MARK MILLAR

Mark and I have worked together before and we got along famously. The thing about that Scorsese comment was, I have a tendency to be more gritty in my depiction of crime and the street drama of New York, and that's what played into Mark's mind. He's told me before that I have that Scorsese look. I think it's just a way of going after my ego and getting me to work with him — which isn't necessary!

I had worked with mainstream comics so much that I didn't ever imagine I would get to do this type of work, but once I began the project, knowing going in that it was going to be R-rated, I was all in. I did have some trepidation but, interestingly enough — and I feel like a hypocrite because I said I wouldn't — then I started enjoying it, and it was an interesting and a strange enjoyment, because of the level of violence, which I had never drawn before. I'd always used discretionary violence in my work. Doing mainstream comic work you typically work towards the teenagers, and you don't want to offend parents because they're the ones who fund the buyers, so you tend to be discretionary. But *Kick-Ass* is all-out, balls-to-the-wall violence. Now here I am, this good old nice guy from New York, a father and a husband, trying to find new and interesting ways to chop people into little pieces.

I've been asked the question, of all the writers I've worked with, who's my favorite, and I have to say Mark. I love the fact that he's from Scotland but he's got a great mainstream American dialogue knack, and he seems to not have a problem with the differences between the two countries, and the vernacular, and the stories.

The true test is when you work with a writer and your art is spurred on by his writing, as opposed to being left to your own wiles. Mark tends to come up with visuals, or sets up the possibility of visuals that are a true help to me, and that's amazing. And I don't say that lightly because very few writers do help out. He's just the full package.

WRITING THE MOVIE SCRIPT

The comic plot was all written, completely planned out, but what we also did was, we had sessions at Matthew's house, where I'd go down and, for the movie script, we'd literally write scenes on cards and block it all out. Normally a comic writer only has minimal involvement in the translation — even when you own the material you basically hand it over — but this was much more like JK Rowling and *Harry Potter*. Matthew did the same thing with Neil Gaiman on *Stardust* as well. He kept me absolutely in the loop at all times.

There were a few little scenes here and there that they'd added into the movie script that I thought, "They're pretty cool," but then unfortunately I ended up not having the space to use them in the comic. The second half of the comic book, issues 5-8, has little things that I nicked from the structure of the screenplay and incorporated into the book though, because it was just so well put together — Matthew's a really brilliant plot guy. And they're not getting a penny for it! But most of it came from chat, and then the co-writer Jane Goldman added in extra stuff again.

Jane added in all these brilliant lines that I wish I'd thought of, and really humanized it a lot more. Her husband's a pal of mine, he's a presenter and chat show host on British TV, Jonathan Ross, and he said that it worked well because my stuff's quite harsh, and Jane really smoothes it out for a mainstream audience and makes the unacceptable somehow acceptable. The same happened on the *Wanted* movie. *Wanted* the book is really dark and really harsh, but through the various drafts of the screenplay the filmmakers made something for a mainstream audience — even though the character is a killer and quite unlikable, you somehow empathize with him a lot more in the movie. Jane's done the same thing for *Kick-Ass*.

SCREENPLAY CO-WRITER *JANE GOLDMAN* ON...

THE CONCEPT

I just loved the idea of *Kick-Ass*. Actually Mark had told me about the idea quite a long time before I read his comic book script. In fact, I'd known Mark before Matthew. I first met Mark — god, I can't remember — I was in my teens, and I don't know how old Mark was. Mark wrote Jonathan a letter back in the late '80s, saying that he was writing *Saviour* and he had a character that was the Antichrist, and wondered if Jonathan would mind if he made him look like him. Mark had thought, if the Antichrist came back, he may well be a popular entertainment figure, and that was at the time when Jonathan broke quite big with his show *The Last Resort*. Anyway, Jonathan was extremely flattered, being a huge comic book fan. So that was the first time our paths crossed.

I could completely understand why Mark was so excited about *Kick-Ass*, because it was such a fresh idea. Although there have been nods to it in comic books before, it's never been explored in the way Mark wanted to explore it, and I was really excited by the idea. I thought it made perfect sense and that the character of Dave was interesting. That's such a fascinating age for guys, that cusp of adulthood. And the idea of comic book fandom, especially living with someone who grew up in that way… I mean, I love comic books, but I didn't start reading them until I was about sixteen, whereas the idea of someone who's grown up obsessing about them was something I totally understood, because it's very much how Jonathan is, and it's always something that I've found very interesting. You know, that idea of escaping to those sorts of worlds, and what effect that would have on you in the real world.

JANE GOLDMAN ON...

THE WORLD OF KICK-ASS

This is meant to be our reality, it's not an alternate reality, it's meant to be very much what would happen if a teenage boy decided to become a superhero in a world where superheroes are our entertainment. We read about superheroes and we watch movies with superheroes in. In a vaguely similar way it's always intrigued me that in zombie films no one ever goes, "Oh my god, it's a zombie uprising!" It's like no one's ever heard of the concept before. In the same way, in superhero films, the tendency is for people to just blindly accept it, but there's no fiction about them and it's not something one aspires to. We liked the idea of saying, "No, this is our universe, where there are comic book fans, but someone decides to become a superhero. So what happens then?" It was an interesting question to all of us.

Basically what we had was Mark's four initial scripts and the structure that took into account where Mark was going with the comic and where Matthew wanted the film to go. It was an unusual situation in that we were essentially adapting something that wasn't even in existence yet. They developed side by side, which was great. Mark's been amazing, in that sense. We were all learning as we went because it really wasn't a straightforward adaptation. Having worked on *Stardust*, where obviously Neil Gaiman was involved — and it was wonderful having his approval and input — but *Stardust* existed and had done for a long time before the adaptation came along, so this was a completely different experience. Mark was absolutely wonderful about it. It was really gratifying, how collaborative it was.

On November 24th at 6.40pm, college student Alex Cerneka was attacked by four men he did not know

He sustained multiple fractures and two stab wounds

while more than fifteen people stood around and watched

LAUNCHING THE COMIC

One of the things that really struck me when I started creating our own stuff was: you're on your own, you have no back-up. If I do something like *Civil War* or *The Ultimates* or *Wolverine*, that has the complete backing of Marvel — getting interviews in *Wizard* magazine, paying for house ads in magazines, doing online campaigns and so on... But this is just me and my pal who's drawing *Kick-Ass*, and it sinks or swims based on the publicity you do for it. In a crowded marketplace of five hundred comics out there every single month, to suddenly appear with a character no one's ever heard of, it's very easy to slink away. Decent sales, decent numbers on a create-your-own book is something like eight, nine thousand copies. That's seen as respectable. I thought, "There's no point doing it if only this number of people are seeing it," so I tried to get a little creative in terms of what I was going to be doing to promote it. I designed an ad that was quite eye-catching. Then I got readers on my message board, who were very kind, to virally put that out all over the internet. I also said, "If people get this printed up and put in comic store windows, we'll give the comic store a free ad in the book. People who virally put the book ad out and talk about the book across the Oprah boards and AOL boards, we'll give them a thank you in the book." So for absolutely no money whatsoever we had this huge campaign across the net, building up anticipation.

The other thing I wanted to do was a viral video, which

KICK-ASS

Hi, my name is Kick-Ass and I'm a real-life superhero. No, that doesn't mean I'm special needs and someone is being patronizing.

Male
21 years old
NEW YORK, New York
United States

Last Login:
12/10/2009

View My: Pics | Videos

Contacting KICK-ASS

video you are about to see
as shot on a camera-phone
student at East Park High
The man in the mask is
a self-proclaimed 'local superhero'
This is the first time
he has been captured on film

He protected Mister Cerneka
for almost eight minutes
until cops arrived
and his attackers fled
Personally, we think
he's pretty AWESOME

York – myspace.com/kickass_comic

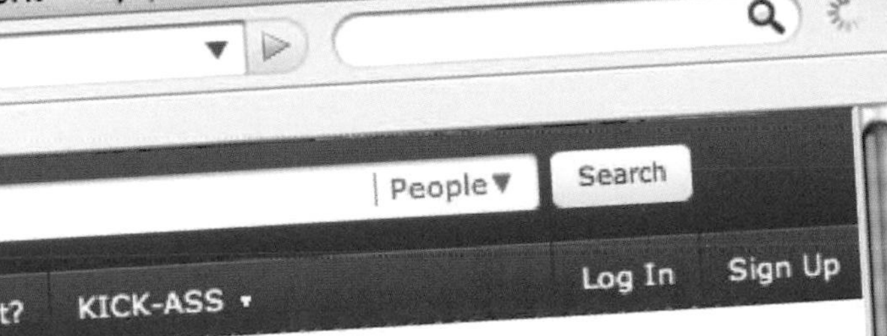
People
Search
Log In
Sign Up
ost?
KICK-ASS
-ASS IS A REAL-LIFE SUPERHERO
Posted at 23:15 19 Dec 2007
view more
atest Blog Entry [Subscribe to this Blog]
DNESDAY IS JUST TWO DAYS AWAY!! (view more)
c gets a Soundtrack (view more)
g Entries]
Blurbs
a masked crime-fighter and work in the Tri-State area of New
life outside of this and so am not available 24/7, but if you
free to leave a message below and I will try to help.

again we'd no money to do. So I got hold of a friend who is out in New York, a filmmaker and ex-Special Forces guy who runs a martial arts class, who's online name is Archonis, and I said to him, "Look, could you do me a favor? Could you put on a mask and get in a fight in a car park, and have a bunch of your pals sort of beat you up and then you beat them up?" And he did it. It looked like someone in the real world, dressing up as a superhero and protecting someone. We put it out on all the message boards. We thought comic fans would be quite into this — the first time that somebody dressed as a superhero is captured on camera — and it went pretty well virally because of that. Again, it was guerilla marketing. We'd absolutely no money to do anything and we just tried to think outside the box a bit.

So it was this massive campaign by the fans really, which was amazing because it just dominated the internet at that time, which never happens outside of a Marvel or a DC event. It became a little event in itself. When they came in, our orders for the first issue were literally six times what we expected. The initial orders were about 60,000, and then subsequently we went through six printings, and we've done over 100,000 of most issues.

I think the first time I realized it was going to be big is when I saw the first issue in black and white, all lettered and printed up, before it had been off to a colorist or anything, and I was just looking through it and I got to the end and I couldn't wait for the next issue. It was weird because it was my book, and I couldn't wait for the next one!

MAKING THE MOVIE

When I read the finished movie script I was thinking, "This is the greatest superhero film I've ever seen in my life. I love it — but nobody's going to make it, the studios are just going to balk."

Matthew said that he was very confident with it though, and he took it to a studio he has a deal with, and they looked at it and said, "We really like it, but can you take out all the violence, all the swearing, and make it a more generic superhero movie?" And he was like, "No, no, I totally believe in the material," which is amazing. The studio said, "Well, we're not prepared to fund it then, because it's a lot of money and we think it's too much of a risk." He was furious at that, quite rightly, and he took it to some other studios and they all said the same thing. I asked, "What do you want to do?" and he said — and this is one of the things that I love about Matthew, that he's a total auteur, he's got balls of brass — he just said, "Look, I believe in it so much that I'm just going to fund it myself. And I like the idea of these guys all having to come back later and say they were wrong." He said, "If these people like it, it's a problem, but if they don't, then usually you're doing something interesting." So, he raised the money, and there were some phone calls and meetings, and then we just started making the film, without a studio.

Matthew likes to surround himself with people who he gets on with, so the same cinematographer's always there, the same production team, it's always the same people coming back. It's almost like a repertory company, they stop working on one movie, maybe go and do other things, and the minute a new movie has come in, they all come together and work on it. Jon Harris, he's the editor on this and he's brilliant, he's been with these guys now for over a decade as well. They're like a family, they bicker sometimes, but everybody's totally watching each other's backs. It's quite amazing to watch them all in action. It's a really good team.

DIRECTOR
MATTHEW VAUGHN ON...

GETTING THE MOVIE MADE

Basically, all of the studios said no to the film. And so quickly. It was weird. I got a hold of some of the studios' coverage [internal feedback on a script] for the project, and the coverage was fantastic. So it was strange that they gave it good coverage but wouldn't engage in the process of even asking what I would do with the film. There was just this knee-jerk reaction to it. Which, in a way, is understandable. The film breaks a lot of taboos, and has certain elements that, if you're a studio executive, might make you think, "Why in the hell would we make a film like this?" One thing I don't think anyone got from the script was how humorous and fun it is. It was hard to understand the tone and the humor and the style of what I was going for. It was very similar to the beginning of the journey for *Lock, Stock* [*and Two Smoking Barrels*], where nobody got the script. They were like, "Is it a gangster film, is it a comedy? What is this? We don't get it! We're not making it!" So we thought, "Fair enough. Screw you guys, we're going to go off and make it."

I can genuinely say what *Lock, Stock* did for gangster movies, we're doing for comic book/superhero films.

PANAV

Opposite above: Jane Goldman on set with Matthew Vaughn.
Opposite below left: Vaughn with director of photography Ben Davis.
Opposite below right: Production designer Russell De Rozario.
Above: Producer Tarquin Pack.
Above right: Mark Millar with actor Mark Strong, who plays mobster Frank D'Amico.

MATTHEW VAUGHN ON... WORKING WITHOUT A STUDIO

My only advice to filmmakers now is "If you don't have any studio involvement, if you have less financial reward or choices, take the less money route. You'll have the time of your life." I had so much fun making this movie. There have been no politics to deal with. I'm not getting notes saying, "Could you make it happy?" or "Could you make it sad?" and then you end up in some horrible nowhere land.

It's really got me so excited about being a director. It was just so *fun*. It's how films should be. Films should be about taking risks and pushing boundaries. The problem with the film business is that it's become too homogenized.

Being a co-producer on the movie felt like a full-time job. If you look, my comic output at that time was quite low because I was spending so much time on the phone or going down to London for meetings. I was involved in everything, from costumes to set pieces to casting. Every night I would type a code into a website and watch that day's casting in Australia, Los Angeles, New York and London, they were casting everywhere. Even background characters, I got input into who was being cast. It was an amazing, quite unique experience in that sense, because it really was a bunch of guys who were friends making a movie, as opposed to a studio being involved in any way. We didn't take any notes from anyone, it was just us.

It's funny because I was a producer on *Wanted*, and all that really meant was they would phone me up occasionally and say, "What do you think of Angelina Jolie being in the film?" "Yes, okay." That's it, that was the kind of conversation I would have. And I would visit the set, but it would be a bit like Prince Charles visiting, where I would go along and nod and smile and meet everyone and then go away again. So with *Kick-Ass* I thought, "Brilliant, more free cash, I'll just go down and visit a few times and that's it." I wasn't expecting it to be so time-consuming. I'm so happy about doing it because it was an amazing experience, to be involved, but it was actually like a job, it was real work. It probably took up about six months of my life, from Christmas-time until we started shooting in the summer really, dealing with it every day. On a small level, Matthew and I would talk on the phone for at least an hour every day, and on the big side I'd maybe spend a week down in London at a time, going into the office or onto the set or something every day. It was brilliant.

I always wondered why nobody did it before me.

This spread and next: Creating the story's opening moments, on the page and on the screen, from the original comic book script to the finished movie scene.

Right: Costume designer Sammy Sheldon's design for the Armenian guy's movie look is very faithful to Romita's comic book original.

KICK-ASS! ISSUE ONE

Script By Mark Millar
Art By John Romita Jr

Page One

1/ Open with a big wide city shot in New York and a tiny figure in a bright costume juxtaposed against this familiar grey cityscape. The reality of this is very important. This is just a guy in a costume standing on the edge of a building.

CAPTION : I always wondered why nobody did it before me.
CAPTION : I mean, all those comic-book movies and television shows you'd think at least ONE eccentric loner would have stitched himself a costume.

2/ Close on this guy and we see him pulling goggles down over his eyes. He's very self-assured and looks quite cool. Very heroic.

CAPTION : Is everyday life really so exciting?
CAPTION : Are schools and offices really so thrilling that I'm the only one who ever FANTASIZED about this?

3/ Pull back as he raises his arms and his wings snap out, the mechanical structure underneath them all looking very realistic.

CAPTION : C'mon. Be honest with yourself.

4/ Shot from above as he gently leaves this roof, his wings on his fists behind him. Again, this all looks very normal for a superhero comic-book.

CAPTION : We all planned to be a superhero at SOME point in our lives.

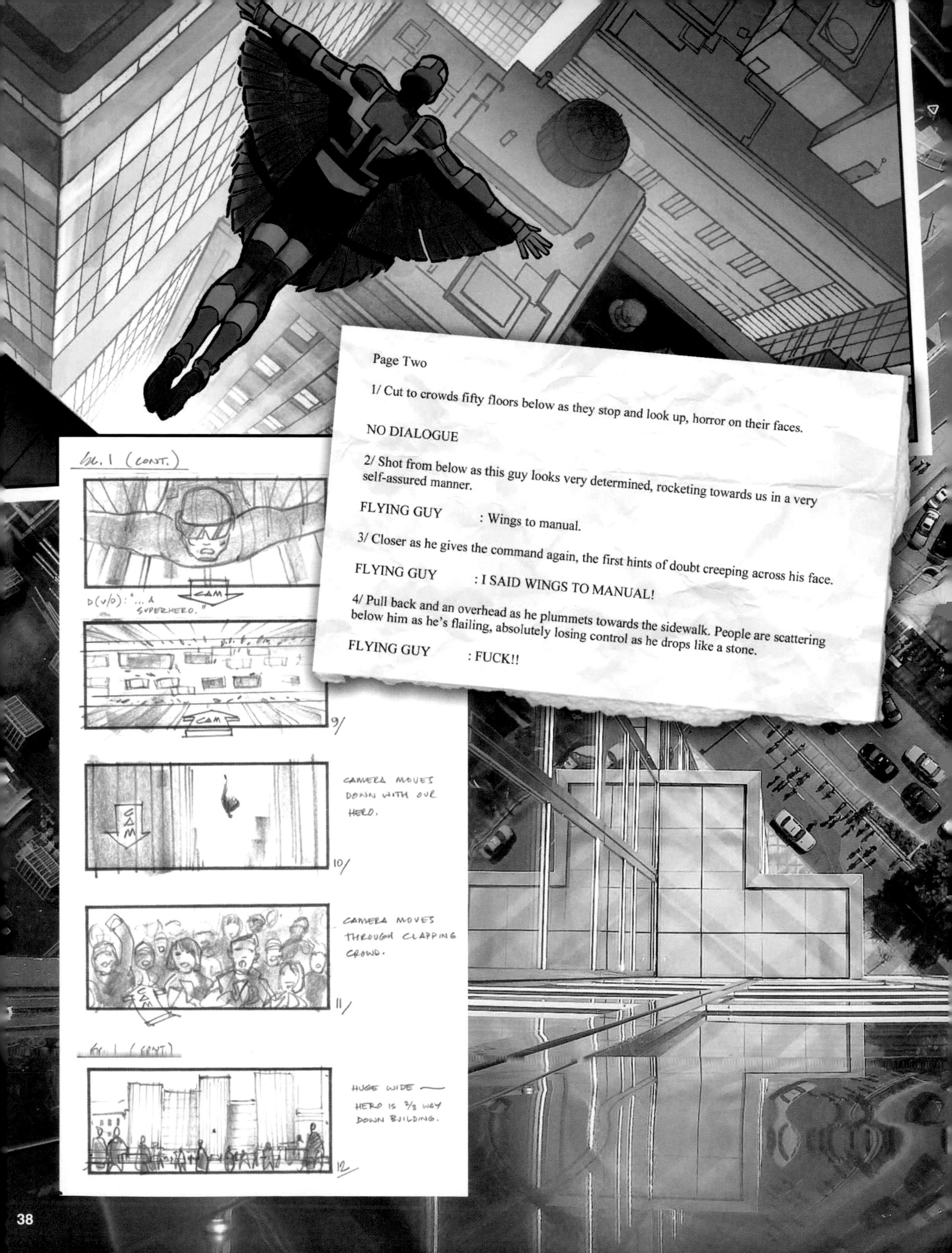

Page Two

1/ Cut to crowds fifty floors below as they stop and look up, horror on their faces.

NO DIALOGUE

2/ Shot from below as this guy looks very determined, rocketing towards us in a very self-assured manner.

FLYING GUY : Wings to manual.

3/ Closer as he gives the command again, the first hints of doubt creeping across his face.

FLYING GUY : I SAID WINGS TO MANUAL!

4/ Pull back and an overhead as he plummets towards the sidewalk. People are scattering below him as he's flailing, absolutely losing control as he drops like a stone.

FLYING GUY : FUCK!!

Sc. 1 (CONT.)
CAM
D(V/O): "... A SUPERHERO."
CAM
9/
CAM
CAMERA MOVES DOWN WITH OUR HERO.
10/
CAM
CAMERA MOVES THROUGH CLAPPING CROWD.
11/
Sc. 1 (CONT.)
HUGE WIDE — HERO IS 2/3 WAY DOWN BUILDING.
12/

ENTERING PRODUCTION

It all happened very quickly. Once we had the script, casting began within weeks, and the movie started shooting a few weeks after that. The thing I hate about the British film scene, and my small experiences of television here as well, is that there are a lot of meetings and nothing happens. That's why I've never been interested in it. Life's too short. The thing I like about Matthew is he doesn't mess about. I would rather just get on with the job, and Matthew's like that, which is great. He simply says, "I love this. Let's do it," and within weeks you've got Nicolas Cage in a costume, saying the lines.

He lands on a PARKED CAR. It crumples like paper. The CAR ALARM strikes up over the crowd noise. We needn't look closer to be sure that he's dead. But what the hell. We track in.

DAVE (V.O.) (CONT'D)

That's not me, by the way. That's some Armenian guy with a history of mental health problems. On the news, his sister said he read about me in the New York Post.

The secret origin of Dave Lizewski:

Occasionally we'll have charity auctions on my website, and to raise money for one particular cause we ended up putting a competition out there. This was before the comic even came out, so we'd nothing really to go on, and it was a leap of faith for anybody that was bidding, but I said, "Listen, we've got a book coming out called *Kick-Ass*. I haven't come up with a name for the titular character yet, his secret identity. If you want to be this guy, you could be the next Peter Parker or John McClane if you start bidding." So for about three thousand dollars this guy Dave Lizewski got to name the character after himself. And it could not be a more difficult name to pronounce and spell! Every time I was writing "Lizewski" I had to go and check it out, because I'd never seen the name before so I didn't have it in my head. The first four issues I spelt it wrong every time — I had to keep going back and changing it.

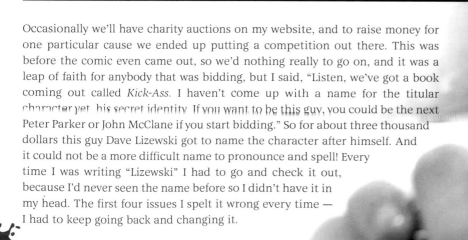

JANE GOLDMAN ON...

DAVE

I know that Mark felt, and Matthew and I completely agreed, that there's no way that this character should be a comedy nerd, he's just a normal kid that we can all relate to. I think the idea of people who are into comic books being especially geeky or socially inept is an outmoded one. It's like saying people who use computers or play console games are geeky — no, we all do it. I think we wanted to take that more modern attitude that he's not a loser, he's just a normal kid. He loves comics and he, as I think we all do at that age, longs for adventure. But he doesn't always think the consequences through, which I think is another typical thing of that age group. I find that age absolutely fascinating, the late teens, because that's the real border between childhood and adulthood — I find that endlessly fascinating.

EXT. HIGH SCHOOL. DAY.

A huge, antiquated building, covered in graffiti. STUDENTS mill around outside. A CAR pulls up and out climbs high school senior DAVID LIZEWSKI. Not quite Napoleon Dynamite, but not quite Zac Efron either.

DAVE (V.O.)

That's me. Back before any of this stuff happened. Back when you'd have to be a lot crazier than that guy to try and be like me.

The casting was a huge thing, because if you have the wrong person in the wrong role it's a disaster. Casting Dave, for example, was an absolute nightmare, because we couldn't find anyone who was charismatic enough. As a kid I always knew that Richie Cunningham and all the people in *Happy Days* were like, thirty-five, and it always looked kind of weird that they were playing teenagers, but now I get it, I know why *American Graffiti* starred a bunch of older actors — it's because teenagers aren't that charismatic, and they generally can't hold a movie together. We discovered the same thing. We looked at some of the biggest young adult actors in the world at the moment. I don't know how many kids we saw. It was twelve weeks of kids every day, to play Dave, and we just couldn't find anyone. Matthew genuinely was going to move the movie back months because he thought, we can't do this movie unless we have a charismatic Dave. Matthew was also quite adamant that he wanted an American actor. Aaron Johnson, who got the part, pretended to be American and did a great screen test, and he got called back, and everybody loved him and he got called back again, and he got the role. It was only at the third screen test, I think, that Aaron admitted that he came from High Wycombe or wherever. It was a real Hollywood-style story — a kid faking being American and wowing everybody. His accent was just bang-on.

Down to the molecules in his hair, he's just exactly what I wanted. It's just like, that's *it*, he's perfect. When I wrote Dave as a comic character and when I see him as a film character, it's all one thing for me.

AARON JOHNSON ON...

BEING CAST AS DAVE

It must have been a really good day because I nailed the accent better than I have before, and Matthew Vaughn was pretty convinced. I also believe that it was just seeing a different face. The casting process had gone on for so long, he'd seen all these people, and I was a fresh face that came in. That's a lot of it. It's all about timing.

The deal was done in two or three days: the audition in the morning, then meeting him at night, the screen test the next day — and at that time I hadn't even read the script. I was fucking nervous as fuck. But I think the screen test was such an improvement on the audition the day before. Then it all happened so quickly. Matthew was in the room, and he said there and then that I'd got the part, but I walked out and called my agents and said, "Well, he said this, but I don't really know..." I was kind of trying to not worry about it.

Dave's bedroom is a typical teenage boy's, down to the discarded tissues...

Aaron Johnson, production sound mixer Simon Hayes, Jane Goldman and Matthew Vaughn on set.

MATTHEW VAUGHN ON...

CASTING AARON

I nearly postponed the movie for a year because I couldn't find Dave. I just couldn't find Kick-Ass. It was a Friday morning, and I said to the guys, "We're going back to London tonight, and we're postponing the movie until we figure out who's playing Dave." Then Mr Aaron Johnson came in, who, mark my words, is going to be a huge movie star. He has that charisma where you believe every word he says. He can also stand in front of the camera and say nothing, but you still want to watch him. The actor I think he'll become is Robert Downey Jr. He's very similar to him.

Sc. 10 INT. HIGH SCHOOL CORRIDOR — DAY.
23.
TRACK BACK WITH DAVE AS HE WALKS DOWN A CORRIDOR.
D(V/O): SURE, A LOT...
CAM
1/
TRACK WITH DAVE, O.T.S. WE APPROACH KATIE DEAUXMA.
CAM
2/
D(V/O): "BUT DON'T GET ME WRONG..."
[AS FR. 1/, TIGHTER]
CONT. TRACK BACK AS HE APPROACHES.
3/
D(V/O): "ESPECIALLY KATIE DEAUXMA."
CAM
[AS FR. 2/, TIGHTER]
KATIE TURNS TO HIM AS HE APPROACHES.
4/
K: "HEY GORGEOUS!"
ERIKA ARRIVES, DAVE TURNS.
5C/
D: "NO, YOU MEANT—ERIKA..."
K: "OH GOD — IT WAS..."
DAVE WALKS MORTIFIED.
WE EASE BACK HIM UNTIL HE CAMERA & EXITS FRAME.
5D/
D: "IT'S COOL..."
"I WAS JUST A REGULAR GUY."

Lyndsy Fonseca plays Dave's object of desire, Katie Deauxma.

JANE GOLDMAN ON...

EVAN AND CLARK

Clark's a great ad-libber, so it was always lovely when he chucked stuff in. He and Evan Peters both have amazing comic timing, and when you get those characters you think, "I wish we had more of this," and then you give them a little bit more time or expand scenes a little bit. Evan's got an incredible dry delivery, and Clark is obviously fabulous. In fact, at the table read, the very first time his part was read, it was immediately obvious that he was the perfect guy for the part. Weirdly, I thought, "Did I actually have Clark in my head when I was writing the lines?" I don't know if I consciously did, because I always try to avoid that, but he made it his own straight away.

Dave's best friend Marty had about eight lines in the movie originally, so we weren't really thinking of anyone especially for the role, we didn't really need to get anyone well-known. Then Clark Duke came in and his screen test [for Marty] was so amazing that I was genuinely laughing, he was ad-libbing bits, so we beefed up his role. Every time he's on camera, you're laughing. He was great. Our idea for *Kick-Ass* — when I was doing the comic, as well as when we went on to the movie — was always *Spider-Man* meets *Superbad*. The humor in superhero movies is normally pretty gentle, it's just nice little jokes. Even things like when Superman catches the helicopter, it's just a gentle joke that he makes with Lois, and you're smiling rather than laughing, that's what superhero humor tends to be like. So I thought, wouldn't it be good if when it's funny it's genuinely funny — as funny as *Superbad* — but then when it's exciting, it's genuinely exciting, and when it's scary, with the gangsters, it should feel like *Goodfellas* or something. It's like a whole bunch of genres all blended into one movie. Clark Duke was perfect for that because he's so naturally funny that he takes the movie to a whole other level.

DAVE
Jesus, doesn't it bug you? Why do thousands of people wanna be Paris Hilton, and nobody wants to be Spiderman?

AARON JOHNSON ON...

ACTING WITH EVAN AND CLARK

Being on set with everybody, there's such great banter and it helps me a lot. With Clark and Evan, when I can jump in with an ad-lib I do, but I tend to end up sitting back just watching them do the scene then think, "Oh fuck, I'm in it, I'm in the scene too!" I mean, concentration is difficult, trying to focus — they've got very dry sarcasm.

CLARK DUKE ON...

BEING A FAN

Matthew didn't really have to pitch *Kick-Ass* to me as I was already a fan of the comic before I even knew they were making a film. Mark Millar is one of my favorite writers in general and I'm a big comic guy since I was a little kid, so I was very aware of it and the thesis of the film — why does everybody want to be Paris Hilton and nobody wants to be Spider-Man? I just thought that was such a killer line, which is in the film too.

With superhero films there seems to be a trend steadily going closer and closer to realism, with this being the next logical step towards that: make it *really* real. It's just a normal kid who tries to be a superhero, but he really gets the shit kicked out of him, backs get broken and stuff, people *die*.

I think a lot of the strength of *Kick-Ass* is it's such a simple idea. When I read the comic I was like, "Shit, why has nobody ever thought of this before?" Those are usually the best ideas, the most obvious ones.

Evan Peters, Aaron Johnson and Clark Duke on the Atomic Comics set.

AT SOME
POINT IN
OUR LIVES, WE ALL
WANTED
TO BE A
SUPERHERO

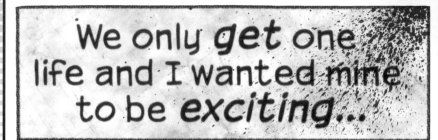

> We only ***get*** one life and I wanted mine to be ***exciting...***

MARK MILLAR ON...

KICK-ASS'S COSTUME

My influence for Kick-Ass's costume was Steve Ditko, because the Steve Ditko *Spider-Man*s were reprinted in the UK when I was about ten, and I remember very clearly Peter Parker sitting on the edge of his bed with a needle and thread sewing his shitty-looking costume together. That always stuck in my mind, that that's what realistic superheroes would be like — your aunt's shouting downstairs, saying your dinner's ready, and you're trying to fix your costume because the Sandman ripped it. And that was a huge influence on *Kick-Ass*. The idea of it being sort of cool, but not *too* cool, was really, really important.

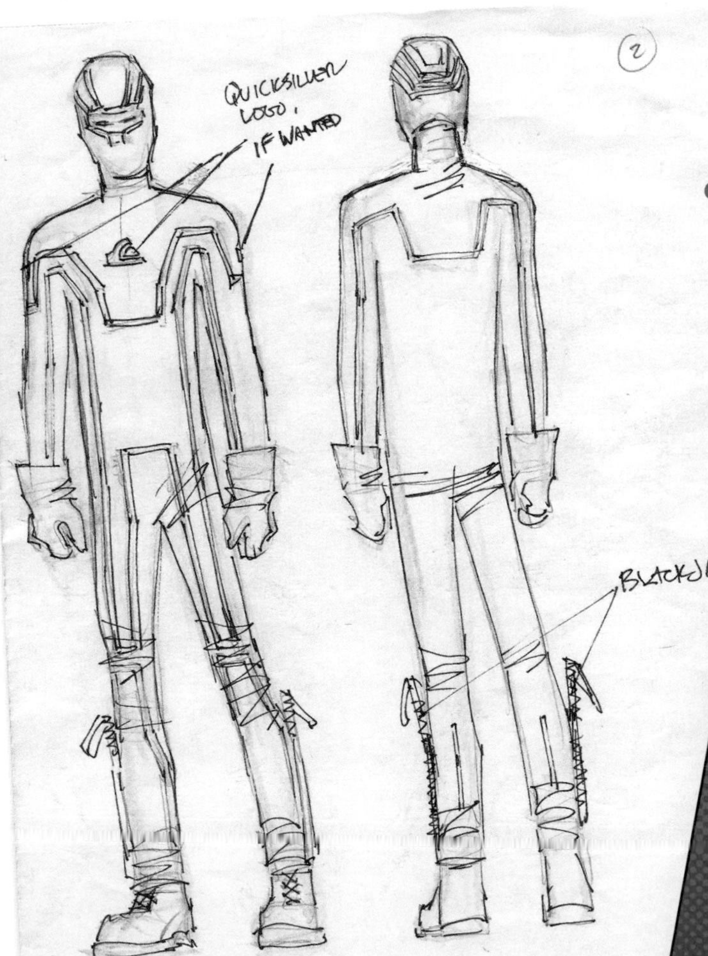

JOHN ROMITA JR. ON...

DESIGNING DAVE

Mark wanted all the costumes to be — and this makes perfect sense — not campy, but to take into account that these are amateur people in the real world that have never put a costume on before or designed a costume, so let them suffer a bit, visually. It's a great little idea, because you would tend to want to make people look heroic in their costumes, and you can't do that with people who are making their own or buying them on eBay. They're going to look silly. We're in the real world, so make them look awkward, make the sixteen-year-old guy look awkward, as if he's uncomfortable in his own costume.

The awkwardness I had no problem with, designing Dave himself, because that's what sixteen-year-olds are, they're awkward, they're uncomfortable, they're not necessarily comfortable socially. So you tend to have hair flopping over the face, cover as much of the face as possible, because there might be acne problems, skin problems, and so on. I looked at styles of kids' hair and at the clothes and at the shapes of sixteen year olds. I couldn't very well go and find fashion magazines for teenagers though, because I'd feel like a strange old man, going into a store and trying to buy children's fashion magazines! My wife picks up magazines that I can look at. So the initial costume was helped out by Mark and Matthew, and the other parts, the everyday discomfort of a sixteen-year-old, I enjoyed throwing that in, because I remember the discomfort I had as a sixteen-year-old.

Back when the original comic scripts had been written and Johnny was doing his first character designs, we were talking about making it a very realistic superhero story. And in reality, chances are you wouldn't put on a costume if you were going to be a vigilante, you'd go out in a hoodie or something — and that's what Johnny drew at first. But it didn't seem right, because the whole idea was that this kid was *so* into comics and that's why he was doing it, so the fetish for him would be dressing up as a superhero. So we went back and forth a little on that, and we involved Matthew as well.

I'd written four issues of the comic before Johnny had started drawing anything, and Matthew agreed he wanted to make the movie before he saw a page of art, so we knew a film was getting made. I wanted to make sure that what we did would translate well into a movie visually, so I said to Matthew, "I've got some sketches here from Johnny. I'll fire them over to you. See what you think," because I wanted it to look good on camera. You know how sometimes, when they make an adaptation, they change the visual and it pisses off the fans? I just wanted to make sure that didn't happen, that Matthew was happy with the visuals. So Matthew came up with the idea of making it a wetsuit that he bought on eBay, and the first drawing Johnny sent of that we loved and just went with — there were no notes whatsoever. It happened very fast and very organically. It was a bunch of like-minded people who were all pretty much on the same page.

INT. DAVE'S BEDROOM. NIGHT.

Dave poses in his costume, flexing his still-tiny pecs.

DAVE (V.O.)
All I knew was I'd never felt so
good about myself.

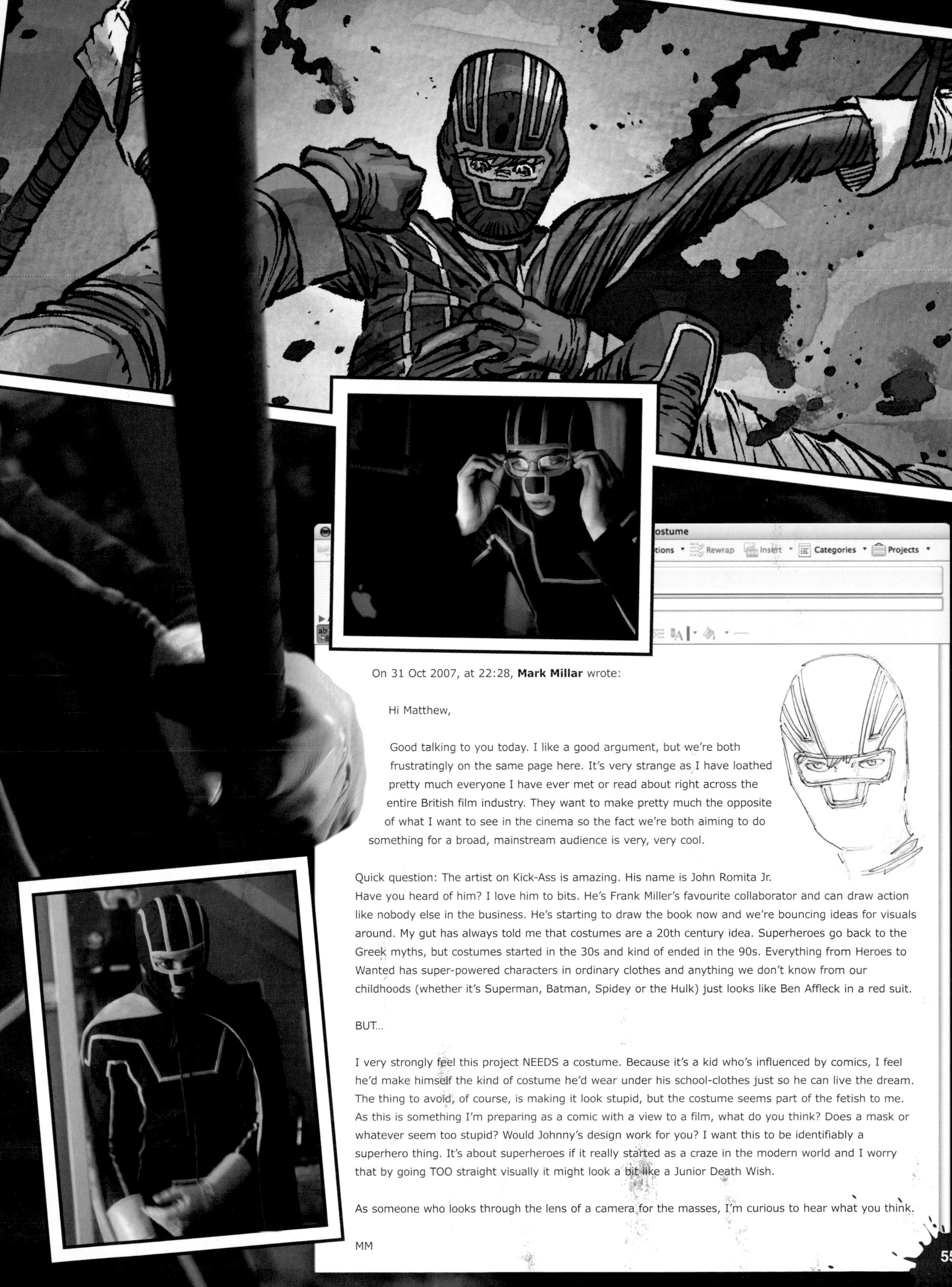

On 31 Oct 2007, at 22:28, **Mark Millar** wrote:

Hi Matthew,

Good talking to you today. I like a good argument, but we're both frustratingly on the same page here. It's very strange as I have loathed pretty much everyone I have ever met or read about right across the entire British film industry. They want to make pretty much the opposite of what I want to see in the cinema so the fact we're both aiming to do something for a broad, mainstream audience is very, very cool.

Quick question: The artist on Kick-Ass is amazing. His name is John Romita Jr. Have you heard of him? I love him to bits. He's Frank Miller's favourite collaborator and can draw action like nobody else in the business. He's starting to draw the book now and we're bouncing ideas for visuals around. My gut has always told me that costumes are a 20th century idea. Superheroes go back to the Greek myths, but costumes started in the 30s and kind of ended in the 90s. Everything from Heroes to Wanted has super-powered characters in ordinary clothes and anything we don't know from our childhoods (whether it's Superman, Batman, Spidey or the Hulk) just looks like Ben Affleck in a red suit.

BUT...

I very strongly feel this project NEEDS a costume. Because it's a kid who's influenced by comics, I feel he'd make himself the kind of costume he'd wear under his school-clothes just so he can live the dream. The thing to avoid, of course, is making it look stupid, but the costume seems part of the fetish to me. As this is something I'm preparing as a comic with a view to a film, what do you think? Does a mask or whatever seem too stupid? Would Johnny's design work for you? I want this to be identifiably a superhero thing. It's about superheroes if it really started as a craze in the modern world and I worry that by going TOO straight visually it might look a bit like a Junior Death Wish.

As someone who looks through the lens of a camera for the masses, I'm curious to hear what you think.

MM

COSTUME DESIGNER
SAMMY SHELDON ON...

THE MOVIE COSTUME

Kick-Ass was kept as faithful to the comic design as possible. The hood was quite a difficult thing to make work though. With a drawing you can make anything work, but when you try and put it onto a body sometimes it doesn't quite fit. It's tricky to take something that's in two dimensions and put it into three dimensions.

Dave is not interested in clothing, so his is functional; it's jeans, T-shirts, that typical American style. We tried to keep the colors very muted — in fact with the whole school we didn't want anything to bounce out — so that when you see the flip side of Dave as Kick-Ass it's so vibrant and quite solid, in sharp contrast to all those muted colors. I'm trying to make a divide between the two worlds.

In essence Kick-Ass's costume is a bright green wetsuit, which is very much the opposite of Dave's look. Dave is really into his comic books and is a little bit reserved. You don't see his body shape in his normal life when he's got layers of clothing on — he probably doesn't want to show that off. Yet the Kick-Ass suit he wears is so streamlined, it's on the edge of being daft; the ankles tucked into the little boots and the tightness of it. I think it's only when you see Kick-Ass in action that the costume looks cool.

EXT. KICKASS ROOF TOP. DAY.

Dave, in his costume, carefully treads the edge of the roof.

DAVE (V.O.)
I'll be honest, there wasn't a whole lotta crime fighting in those first few weeks.

He reaches the corner and looks across to the next rooftop. He glances down into the narrow alleyway separating the two.

AARON JOHNSON ON...

BEING IN COSTUME

At first I don't know if I felt like a superhero or just an idiot in the costume. But it's funny, I was in Toronto and shooting a lot of the location stuff and I'd get, "Go, go Power Rangers" and "Kermit the Frog" and "Gummy Bear" and stuff like that, so I'm dreading what I might get when it comes out. Or "Gimp", I'm the gimp.

MARK MILLAR ON...

FIGHTING

Kick-Ass didn't really have any fighting skills, so I had to give him something that he could use against bad guys. Obviously he couldn't use a gun because he was a superhero fan so he wasn't going out to kill people, but big sticks just seemed like the logical choice. The idea of two iron bars seemed like the perfect weapon for him — it's not sophisticated, they can't do anything special, you just hit people over the head with them and hopefully not kill them, and that was it. It was as unsophisticated as that. Again, it comes from this plan I had when I was about fifteen. That was our idea — we were going to have one stick each for beating people with. Thank God that never happened, or I'd be writing comics from prison by now.

```
Without warning, the first kid steps up and punches Dave.

Dave reels. But now we see that, behind his back, he has a
piece of LEAD PIPE. He cracks it over the kid's head. The
kid goes down, the screwdriver flying from his hand.

A beat. Then the second kid sets on Dave. The pipe gives
Dave an initial advantage. But now the first guy is up
again.
```

MR. LIZEWSKI
still have that met
tor at your scho
DAVE
It'

...ts these as...

...ve's hospital...

DAVE

How cool is this? I look like Wolverine.

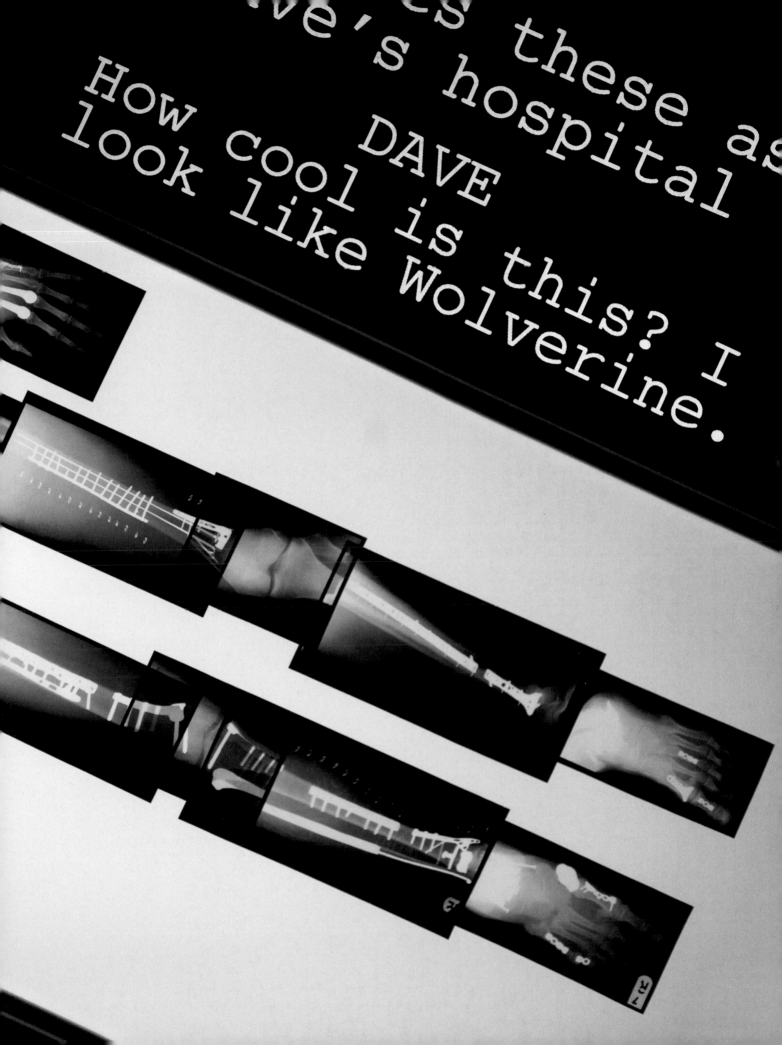

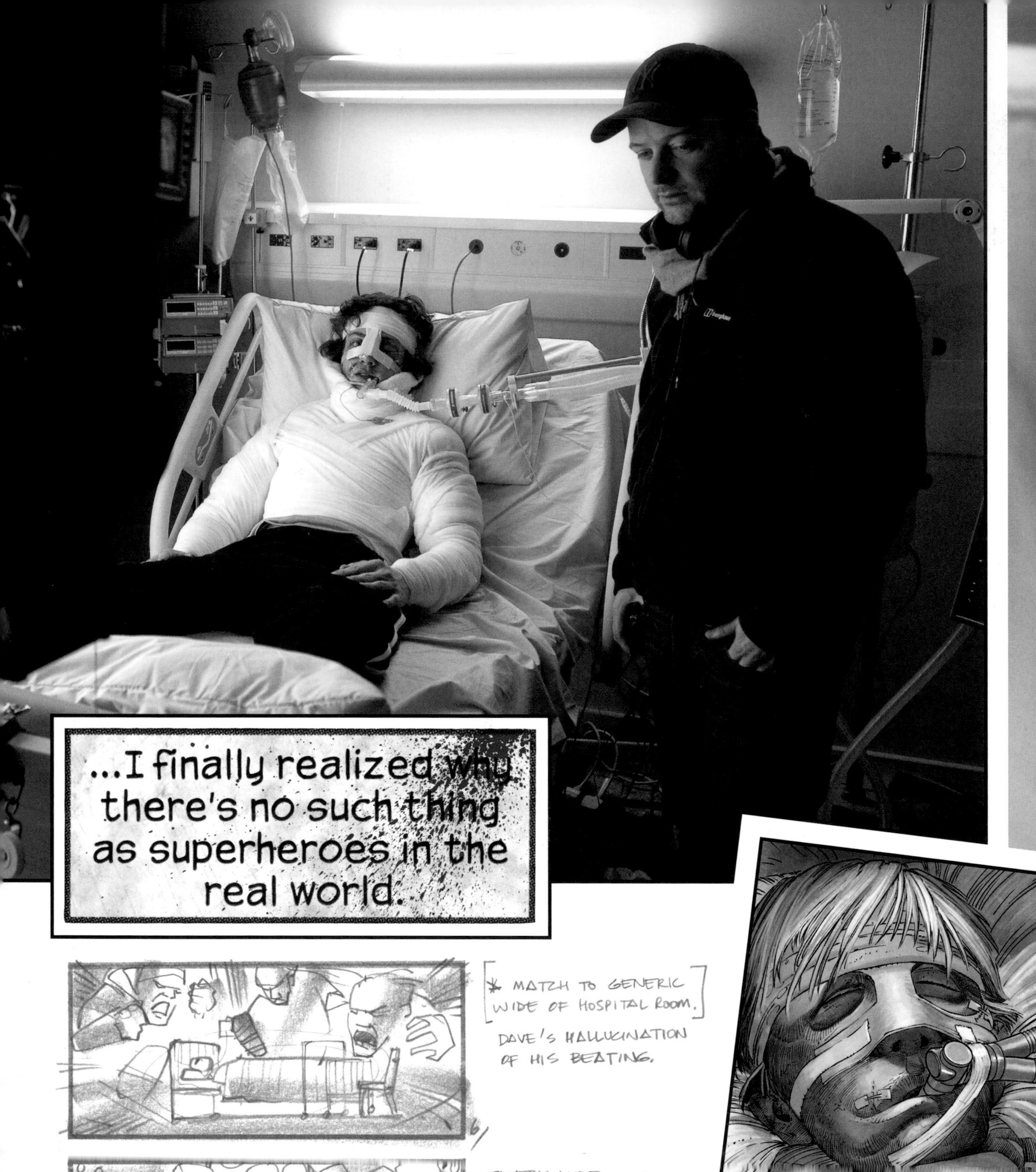

...I finally realized why there's no such thing as superheroes in the real world.
* MATCH TO GENERIC WIDE OF HOSPITAL ROOM.
DAVE'S HALLUCINATION OF HIS BEATING.
6/
GENERIC WIDE —
DAVE'S SURGERY HALLUCINATION.
7/

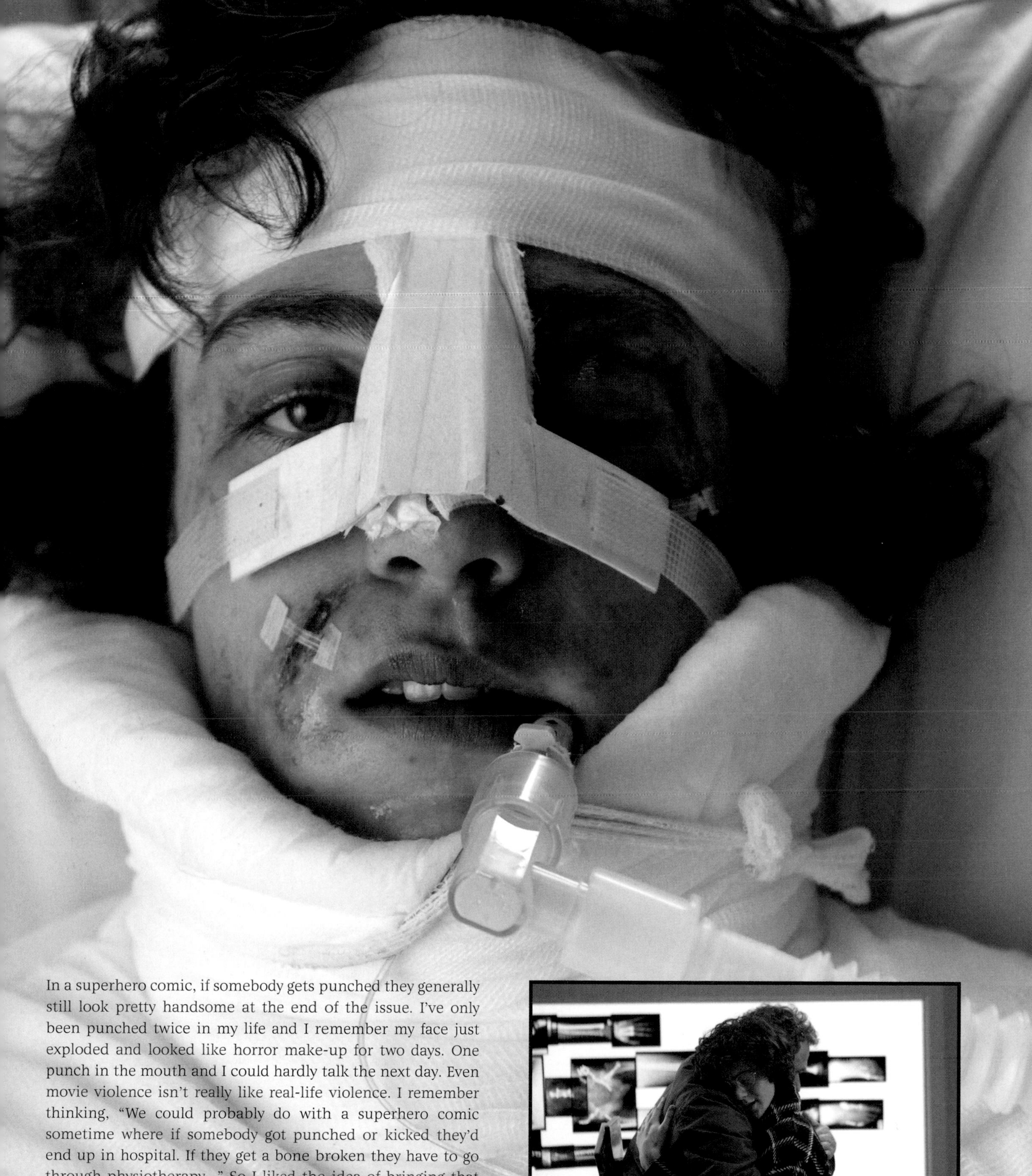

In a superhero comic, if somebody gets punched they generally still look pretty handsome at the end of the issue. I've only been punched twice in my life and I remember my face just exploded and looked like horror make-up for two days. One punch in the mouth and I could hardly talk the next day. Even movie violence isn't really like real-life violence. I remember thinking, "We could probably do with a superhero comic sometime where if somebody got punched or kicked they'd end up in hospital. If they get a bone broken they have to go through physiotherapy..." So I liked the idea of bringing that attitude to superhero comics, because nobody had ever done that before. So with Kick-Ass's first night out on patrol where he gets stabbed and run over by a car, I wanted him in hospital for months and his family left with a lot of bills, and him seeing a psychiatrist and a physiotherapist — all the things that would come with genuine violence.

BIGGEST GUY (CONT'D)
outta here! This
ain't none of your business.
DAVE
Yeah, it is.
his lead pipe and piles in, blazing, taking hits
and centre and landing plenty of his own.
slow down to gawp. Dave shouts to them.
DAVE (CONT'D)
Somebody call 911!

JANE GOLDMAN ON...

KICK-ASS'S FAME

After Dave's first abortive attempt at fighting crime he doesn't give up. He comes back and he finds himself in a situation where he actually ends up successfully protecting another guy from an attack, which happens to be shot on a camera phone — which I thought was a genius idea of Mark's because that completely reflects everything that happens today. Of course it winds up on YouTube and he becomes a YouTube celebrity overnight, which results in him actually having people approach him to help them fight crime and to deal with their problems, which means that his small backyard adventure suddenly explodes into being something much larger. But it's just sheer fate or bad luck that he winds up, on one of the very first outings he makes, being drawn into this much larger and much darker, absolutely deadly plot that's going on.

EXT. HOUSING PROJECT. NIGHT.

Dave - in costume - walks the street. A few KIDS cheer as he passes. Some NO-GOOD TYPES cross the street nervously. A SHADY-LOOKING GUY unexpectedly high-fives him.

DAVE (V.O.)
I don't know if I was everything Katie had always dreamed her gay b.f.f. would be. But I tried my best. And, more importantly, I talked her into mailing Kickass.

At a nasty block, he pushes bells 'til someone buzzes him in.

DAVE (V.O.) (CONT'D)
Long story short, this particular lame duck of hers had turned out to be more of a lame cobra.

MARK MILLAR ON...

BEING ON SET

You feel slightly removed from it, because there's a part of your brain that feels it's not really happening. I found that on the *Wanted* set. I was in Wesley's bedroom on *Wanted*, James McAvoy's room, and they'd laid it out the way J.G. Jones had drawn it in the comic — the bedside cabinet was the same, the clock was the same — and it was weird walking around something in three dimensions that not only had existed in two dimensions when you last saw it, but had only existed in your head a little while before that. It was odd, it was like walking around inside one of your own dreams, but you could touch things. It was even more so on *Kick-Ass*, because they were so faithful to the comic. It was like a dream that was going on forever, weeks and weeks. I went to the set and there it was, men working in the background, making something that should be just a thought into something solid. On that level, you almost can't comprehend it, when you're walking round and you see someone in a costume that you just saw as a sketch, thinking about their lines and ready to walk on and play a part, and there's somebody else dressed as another character you made up and they're referring to each other by the name that you *might* have called something else. It is quite a surreal experience, and you can't entirely appreciate it until it's happening in front of you.

The strangest thing is, you feel fiercely protective of everyone, because on some level you feel as if they're your kids or something. It's like creating a new human being in a sense, the way you do when you're creating a child — you hope everybody likes them and everything's going to work out well for them. I felt quite paternal about Chloë Moretz in particular. We got on really well, we sat together on the side of the camera when she was not on scene, and we'd just chat.

Rasul's apartment, from original comic panel to finished set.

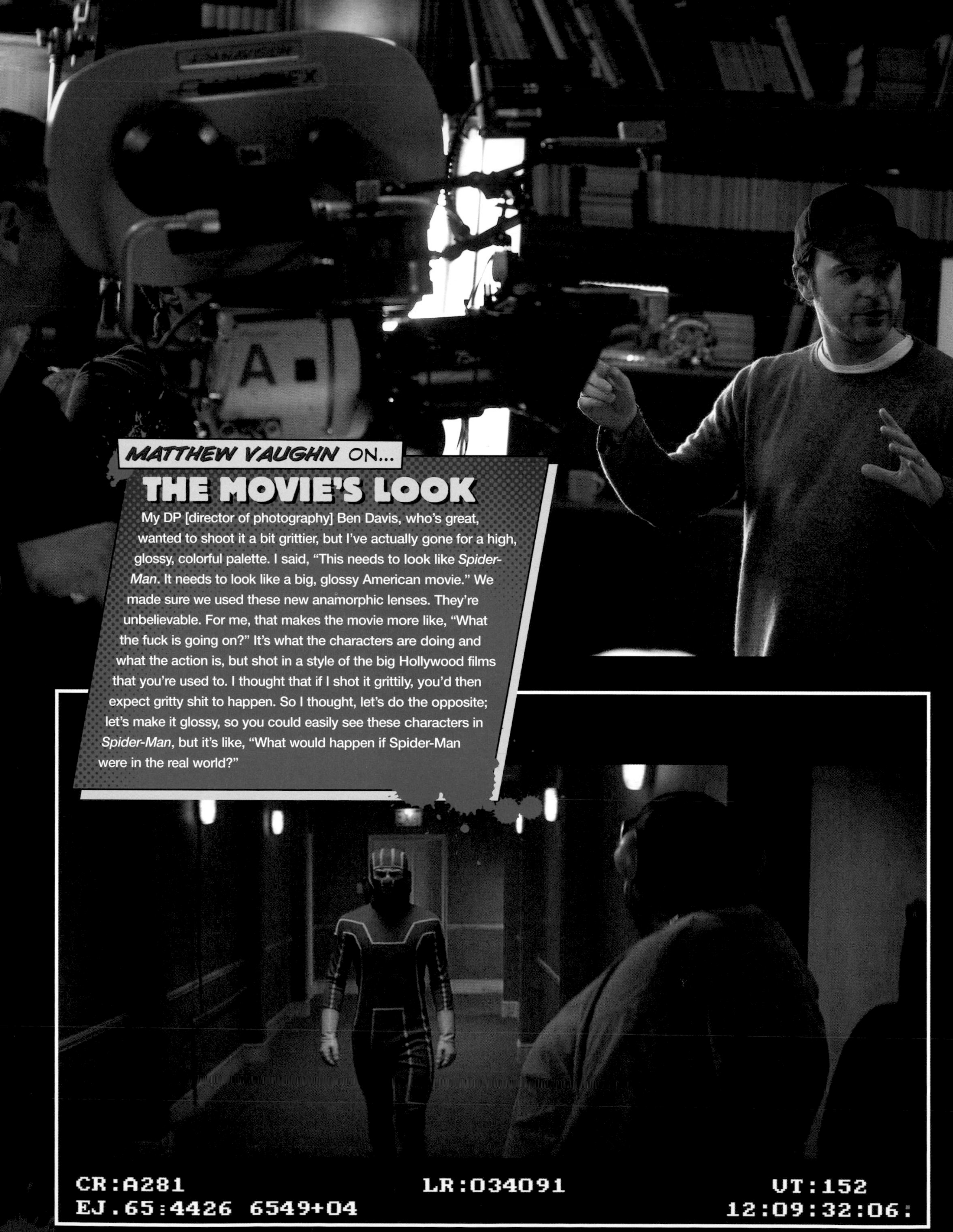

MATTHEW VAUGHN ON...

THE MOVIE'S LOOK

My DP [director of photography] Ben Davis, who's great, wanted to shoot it a bit grittier, but I've actually gone for a high, glossy, colorful palette. I said, "This needs to look like *Spider-Man*. It needs to look like a big, glossy American movie." We made sure we used these new anamorphic lenses. They're unbelievable. For me, that makes the movie more like, "What the fuck is going on?" It's what the characters are doing and what the action is, but shot in a style of the big Hollywood films that you're used to. I thought that if I shot it grittily, you'd then expect gritty shit to happen. So I thought, let's do the opposite; let's make it glossy, so you could easily see these characters in *Spider-Man*, but it's like, "What would happen if Spider-Man were in the real world?"

SAMMY SHELDON ON...

SUPERHERO COSTUMES

We wanted to make the superhero costumes believable, not made from other-worldly fabrics. They have to be grounded in stuff that we know and in a style that is relevant to each character. Matthew wanted their designs to spring from how each of the characters would see themselves as a superhero.

All the colors in the night-time, superheroes' world are very jewel-like, the silhouettes are very strong, there's nothing hazy about the edge of each character. So in the daytime all the kids at school just merge together in a melee of grays and pale colors, and then you have Red Mist in his car and Kick-Ass's green suit. Even Hit-Girl's costume makes a strong impact, though there aren't a lot of colors in it.

OKAY, YOU CUNTS.
LET'S SEE WHAT YOU CAN DO.

She was like John Rambo meets Polly Pocket.

Hit-Girl was another problematic casting and we were having real trouble finding someone. Then from heaven Chloë descended and was just perfect. It was like Jodie Foster circa 1976 walking in — we were like, "Oh my god!" This tiny person with that much attitude, who swore so convincingly, she seemed like a tiny female Joe Pesci! Everybody was just looking at each other: "This is the one. This is who it's gotta be." Kick-Ass and Hit-Girl were the two linchpins of the whole movie — from there it got quite easy, but if those two had been cast wrong it would have been a disaster, because they were our Luke Skywalker and our Han Solo, we absolutely had to get them right. After that everyone else just fell into place.

Above: Early Romita sketches for Hit-Girl.

JOHN ROMITA JR. ON...

HIT-GIRL'S COMIC COSTUME

I had something slightly different with the first designs for Hit-Girl — the first sketches were a leather coat and her mask and tight boots and the jeans. But Mark and Matthew wanted a costume with a cape, because again, she wants to be a superhero, that's the whole idea. He reads comics, the father, they understand comics and they want to look like superheroes, even if they are vigilantes. Then we just did a bit of back and forth on the costume. Give her a mask, let her hair show so you can see it's a little girl, and cape and boots. I came up with the idea for the katanas — the martial arts swords — my son and I were taking Jujitsu lessons, and I saw kids in the class that were just prodigies and were doing things at six and seven that could kill adults, so I imagine that's entirely possible, for this little girl to be a vigilante maniac with swords that can slice people into little pieces.

MARK MILLAR ON...

CHLOË MORETZ

Chloë's interesting because she seems, she looks like a child, but there's this adult brain in there. Jodie Foster's the person we keep comparing her to — she has a career plan and things like that. You do feel as if you're talking to another adult when you're talking to her, but she's still charming and funny at the same time. She and Nic Cage really clicked, which is good because the chemistry between the two of them's really important.

On 8 Sep 2008, at 17:57, **Matthew Vaughn** wrote:

What do you think, it's this or natural pig tails...

On 8 Sep 2008, at 18:05, **Mark Millar** wrote:

> Pink's been done in three other quite iconic films, green is too alien and white makes her look like Storm from the X-Men. I like blue, but LOVE the purple. It just feels new, works better at night (she wouldn't want a bright colour working in the dark) and it goes with the costume. Altogether, that's an iconic look I love. Plus in the comic she has a black wig she slips off for blonde hair under and this would match really well. Black too dull for film, but purple would be amazing.
>
> PS Yesterday and Sat bloody great. Had a great time and home totally buzzing about this. It's going to be massive. I have total, unblinking, almost insane faith in this project.

SAMMY SHELDON ON...

HIT-GIRL'S MOVIE COSTUME

Hit-Girl and Big Daddy's costumes were designed on a tactical level, in that they were weapon related. Hit-Girl had already appeared in the second issue of the comic book, so we kept the color, but I added lots of bits and pieces so [in the movie] she's wearing a child's biking outfit that's been adapted to give it an oriental flavor and be more functional. Keeping in mind that the dad made this for his kid so it's got to have an edge to it that's fun, the fabrics that we chose, lots of leather, have a texture which suggests a fantasy element — its got a shiny pearlized surface — and we added a little kilt to keep it a bit feminine.

It's an extraordinary sight as this tiny, lethal figure flies between the two, knives flashing, deflecting every blow as she slices and dices these two guys three times her size.

Once they're down, she pulls the knife from Rasul's back and stares at Dave. Terrified, he aims his taser at her.

MINDY (CONT'D)
Dude, that is one gay-lookin'
taser.
(a beat)
Chill. We're on the same team.

MARK MILLAR ON...

HIT-GIRL

This will sound so unfair to Kick-Ass, but my favorite moments are probably the Hit-Girl moments. Maybe my favorite sequence of all is when all those drug guys are going to kill Kick-Ass, and until that moment you don't realize he's got anyone that can possibly help him, so he's in a very desperate situation, he's absolutely buggered, and then her appearance is so strong — when you see her for the first time — and the fact that she swears when she appears... She's just killed a man, and swears, and she's tiny! I think the impact of that is amazing. Then before you can catch your breath you see her wiping everyone out. It's startling to watch.

MATTHEW VAUGHN ON...

CHLOË MORETZ

I will bet you any amount of money you want, anything at any odds, I'll give you a million-to-one odds if you want, that you will a) fall in love with Chloë, b) buy her, and c) think, "My god, I just saw the Jodie Foster/ Natalie Portman of this generation."

As for the swearing... we actually had a swearing ban in the house when I grew up. It was a traditionally Catholic household. It wasn't strict in that sense, but there was just a level of respect everyone had, that nobody ever swore at home. To this day. I've got four brothers and one sister — I've never heard any of them swear. I remember hearing my dad saying "arse" once, when I was about nine, and I was quite shocked, because it was just not done in the house! And that's a habit I've carried on. I can think of nothing worse than hearing your kid swear. Maybe that's why it seemed extra funny, the idea of doing it as a character.

MINDY
C'mon, asshole. Can't use the front door now.

When I was trying to kick off my career, my work was a bit Silver-Agey. Then, just before my daughter was born, one of my friends said to me, "Oh, I hope your stuff still has some kind of edge when you have a kid," and I said, "What do you mean?" He said, "Well, Ian McEwan went soft after his kid was born. Having a child humanizes everyone." So from the moment my daughter was born, in 1998, my work got really severe, it got a lot harder. I started purposely making my stuff *more* bad taste so that people couldn't accuse me of that.

It's funny, in comics we live in our own little cocooned world. Stuff people like Garth Ennis and Warren Ellis are doing, if that was appearing out there in the mainstream on a soap opera like *Coronation Street* or something, people would be losing their minds. It's a pretty sheltered world in comics, it's like we can do anything we like. And that's great, because it gives you this creative license to do what you want. But I'm starting to realize, now that I've crossed over into the mainstream a little bit, things could get quite interesting. The kind of stuff we're not that bothered about in comics would cause a furor, and there are certain sections of the press here in the UK that are probably going to pounce on it. The combination of violence, children, and a superhero costume is very potent, because you relax when you see a child, and you assume nothing too bad's going to happen. You relax even further when you see a superhero costume, because that in your subconscious symbolizes safety. And then when you see what this kid is going to do, in a superhero suit — I think it's going to blow people's minds. Even now, a year on from having written those scenes, I'm shocked when I look back at them sometimes, it's quite startling. And if *I'm* shocked, I think once it hits the mainstream it's going to be ten times more powerful.

On the plus side, I think we've created an icon. I actually think Hit-Girl is going to be the movie's Han Solo, is going to be the breakaway thing that's going to be massive. I can see spin-off movies.

Finder File Edit View Go Window Help

ChloeMoretz.com | Suppor

   http://www.chloemoretz.com/

Hit-Girl's Blog!

As featured on **www.chloemoretz.com**

August, 2008 + It's Official....I'm Hit Girl!!!!!!!!

Holla! I can now announce to you that I am officially Hit Girl in the upcoming film Kick Ass. I get to play a really cool action character named Hit Girl. I worked really hard to get the role and I am going to have to work even harder now. I started martial arts training this weekend and it is sooooooooooooo much fun. I love it!

September, 2008 + Hit Girl Checking in! LOL!!!!!!!!!

Wow! Wow! Wow! I know, my mom would kill me cause she would say I need to use a bigger vocabulary but all I can say is WOW! I had my final wardrobe, make up, and hair screen test for Hit Girl and I can't believe it. It is the way coolest suit I have ever seen! I'm not kidding. Wait till you see it. I can't say anything about what it looks like but just let me say it is the coooooooooolest Super Hero Girl EVER! You won't recognize me in it. It feels so fun when I put it on. It's like I just become Hit Girl and not Chloë. She is going to be sooooooooo kick butt! I wish you guys would be able to see it when it comes out on film but its gonna be rated R so most of yall won't get to.

My training is killing me but it is great. The stunt guys are amazing. I have learned to do so many things it's ridiculous! I'm gonna come back to LA like Superwoman or something. I can do like 12 chin ups and 30 push ups and 65 crunches. I can do back handsprings and a whole bunch of other stuff that I couldn't do before this film.

I haven't gotten my finished Hit Girl costume yet. I've had several fittings and it is going to ROCK! Just wait, Hit Girl is so BAAAAADDDDD! She is going to be so cool (probably too cool for me! Haha) but I cannot wait to get in the final costume with full hair and makeup and see what I look like. This film is going to ROCK! The writer (Jane Goldman) is the COOLEST lady I've ever met. She wears the coolest clothes and her hair is bright PINK! I love it! She just keeps making the script better and better. The cool part is that so many people are working on this script, Matthew, Jane and Mark and it is sooooooooooooo good. The comic books have almost all sold out (I've been told) but I have all 4!

I got to see Mark Millar the other day on set. He is the guy who writes the Kick Ass comic. He is so cool. He has this funny Scottish accent. I can't do the accent but I wish I could. I do a pretty good British accent but Scottish is just crazy! I still can't believe what a cool role he wrote for an 11 year old. Everyday, I just get to go to set and do all this stuff that is like something Angelina Jolie would do in a movie.

Done

Fri 16:47

Grace Moretz since 2005

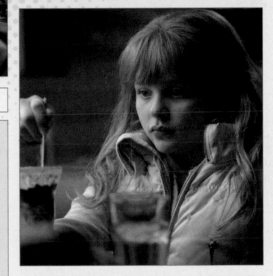

November 2008 + S'up peeps?

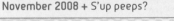

I lost something on my film Kick Ass...MY TEETH!

Hi everybody. Chloë's in da house. oh yea. I'm still having a blast. I have been shooting non stop action sequences for the past five days and it ROCKS! I'm shooting and jumping and doing crazy things. I killed a whole bunch of bad guys today, well Hit Girl "killed" them. These guys are so sweet though. They all stay in a big room right next to my dressing room and then they come down to set and I have to kill them off! It's crazy. I tell you, it's gonna be pretty hard to find another film that is going to be this fun and action packed. I have not met anyone on the film that is not loving it. I do have some interesting news from the set. I lost 2 teeth in the past 5 days. It's so cool. I lost one of my upper molars and 3 days later I lost another one. I lost the first one when I was on my way to set and I lost the second one while I was sitting in the make up chair becoming Hit Girl. I laughed so hard when my tooth fell out. It was awesome. 2 teeth in one week. I have not gotten the chance to leave them under my pillow for the tooth fairy yet because they are in my mom's purse. I need to do that tonight or tomorrow because I could use the cash! Ha, ha. No really, I wonder how much 2 teeth will bring me. I'll let you know when the tooth fairy visits. I was laughing after I lost the second tooth and saying that I should pretend that they got knocked off onset while I was fighting the bad guys. Maybe I should still do that. It wouldn't be any fun to do that now though because I couldn't fake the blood.

John Romita drew me a super cool pencil drawing of me in my Hit Girl uniform and signed it and I screamed for like an hour!! My mom is having it framed so that I'll have it alway and forever.

Always remember..................
Y'ALL ROCK!!!
Chloë Grace xoxoxoxoxoxoxoxoxoxoxoxxoxoxoxoxoxoxoxoxoxo

SC. 84 (CONT.)
4.
DAVE'S P.O.V. AS MINDY RUNS TO THE 1ST PARAPET.
WE SEE BIG DADDY IN B/G.
CAMERA MOVES FORWARDS...
8A/
CAM
...TO SEE MINDY LEAP/SOMERSAULT OFF THE TOP ROOF...
M.
8B/
CAM
... + LAND ON THE LOWER ROOF. SHE FORWARD ROLLS TO THE LEDGE.
8C/
CUT INTO TIGHT PROFILE.
MINDY
CAM
9/

Hit-Girl leaps, from Romita's original comic book art via storyboards to the final shoot. The poster behind Big Daddy features a cameo from the director's wife.

BD

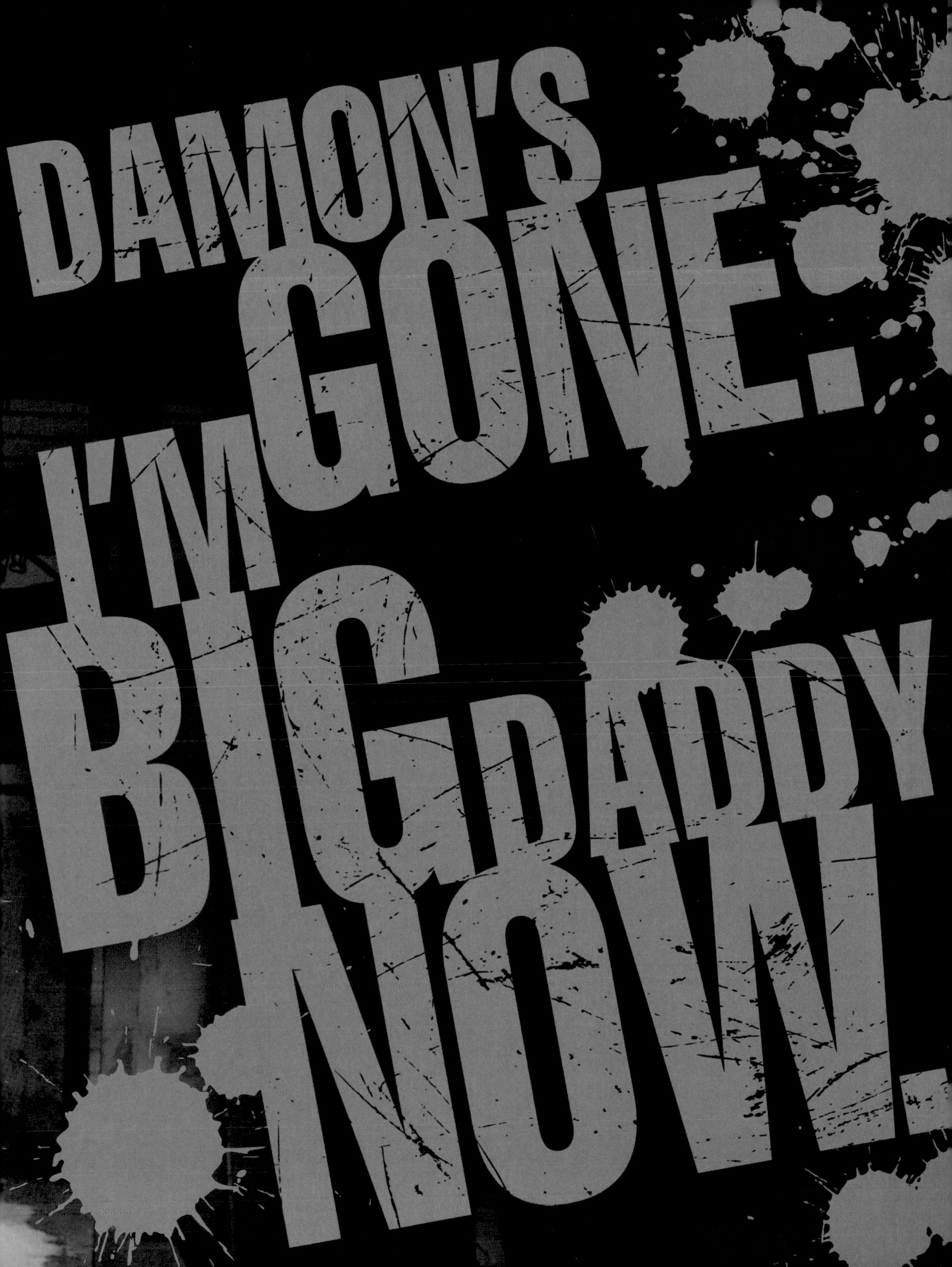
DAMON'S
GONE:
I'M
BIG
DADDY
NOW.

...Dad tells me everything
I need to know.

We knew it was going to be an A-list actor for Big Daddy, we knew somebody who was really good would pull it off. We'd talked about a few people, but although we never considered him initially, now we can't imagine anyone other than Nicolas Cage doing it, and we love the idea.

But even though we were considering other people for the movie, when I was writing the dialogue in the comic book scripts, especially when he's in his secret identity, I had Cage in mind for the delivery style for some reason — it was just that way Cage talks, that was the voice I had in my head when I was writing it. And it was so weird, because in the script for issue 6 I actually wrote, as a note for Johnny, "In terms of delivery, think a dry, laconic Nicolas Cage." I wrote that before Cage had been cast. I just read it again the other day, and I was actually quite shocked — it was almost like subconsciously I knew it was going to be him. But it was totally unintentional.

Cage brought a huge thing to the Big Daddy character that I absolutely loved. It was the idea that this guy is such a fanboy that whenever he puts on the suit he speaks with the stilted staccato delivery of Adam West, which is amazing. It was Matthew who came up with my favorite detail in the movie, that in Damon's secret identity he's got quite a small mustache, but whenever he becomes Big Daddy he puts a larger mustache on to disguise who he is! I thought that was just brilliant.

That was my first experience of an actor bringing something to a performance that would make it a hundred times better. In comics, it's just black and white words in balloons; the subtleties that a great actor can bring aren't there in a comic book. I had simply seen it as dialogue, but when he brought that little extra thing to it I realized, "Ah, *that's* why these guys get paid." The Adam West thing is amazing, because I love the idea of taking what in comics we would call Silver Age ideas, the idea of superheroes being these larger-than-life, colorful, nice characters, and then juxtaposing that with extreme violence. We expect to see Joe Pesci kill a guy, but we don't expect to see a tiny girl in a superhero suit doing it, and similarly Nic makes you relax by talking like Adam West — but there's something weird in his eyes that looks like a crazy person, and it took the character to a whole different level.

He was the first guy on the set every day, and the last guy to leave, staying around for hours after he was done filming. There wasn't any of this going back to your trailer, he was sitting with headphones on watching other people's performances and was just absorbed in it. This is a guy that, when he commits to something, he throws himself into it a thousand per cent.

NICOLAS CAGE ON...

KICK-ASS

The script came to me and I was offered Frank D'Amico. I didn't want to play Frank D'Amico, but then I found out that Matthew had offered me both parts, Damon and D'Amico, so I looked back at the script and read it again and thought, "You know what, Damon and Mindy are the heart of the movie in my opinion, that's where the love is," and that's what was interesting to me about it.

I didn't see the comic until I got here and I saw what Mark had gotten up to. I like Mark, I think he's a great guy, he's been on the set and all that, but it did spook me! I was like, "Are we going to be doing *that* in the movie?"

MARK MILLAR ON...

ROMITA'S BIG DADDY

Johnny needed to draw a page with Big Daddy on it — I think it was issue 4 — but Matthew hadn't cleared anything yet, because he wanted his designer to be involved for Big Daddy. I said, "Look, we don't have time to hang around, Johnny has to draw it." So Johnny went ahead and drew his version, which I think works well for the comic.

JOHN ROMITA JR. ON...

BIG DADDY'S COMIC COSTUME

What I wanted to do was to have the body armor shape to protect Big Daddy from all the gunfire, and I thought of him being an ex-con, that he would do that kind of thing, and having the overcoat to protect him from more of that. Mark said, "Have the face covered up," because that's what somebody would do, they would try to keep their privacy and be anonymous. I threw in the big heavy overcoat, to make it look more realistic. Then, with having the Kevlar, I tried to give it a bit of a leather biker-type look.

SAMMY SHELDON ON...

BIG DADDY'S MOVIE COSTUME

Big Daddy's costume is very tactical. We didn't want to make it purely superhero, it has a practicality to it. Of all the superheroes, he's the one that is most grounded in where he's going, in what his mission is — there's a single reason for what he's doing, so his stuff is very practical.

Big Daddy's helmet is cast from Nicolas Cage's head, and it had to be as close fitting as possible so that it didn't look like it was a crash helmet. One of the things that Matthew was very keen on was keeping the bottom half of Big Daddy's head free so that you can see this big handlebar mustache.

NICOLAS CAGE ON...

MATTHEW VAUGHN

The thing that I like best about Matthew, outside of being a nice guy and I enjoy his company, is he's very interested in doing original, artistic work and he likes similar artists that I like. He likes Keith Haring and Andy Warhol, so I got this feeling that we were going to do some sort of pop-art movie that would hopefully be like this Grand Guignol version of a Lichtenstein or something.

MARK MILLAR ON...

FANBOYS

I said to Cage on the first day of shooting that this is a movie about fanboys, made by fanboys, and I think it's got a weird sincerity because of that. Cage has an amazing comic book collection and his stage name is taken from a comic book character. Then there's me, there's Matthew, Jane is married to Britain's most famous fanboy — Jonathan has the best collection of comics in Britain, and I *think* he's got the best collection of original comic art in the world. So it's a very cultish group of people who really, really love what they're doing, making this film.

NICOLAS CAGE ON...

ADAM WEST

To me there will only be one Batman and that's Adam West. I didn't want to dwell too much on it, but remembering Adam West, and particularly his delivery, I wanted it to feel like it had made such an impact on Damon that, as he lost his mind, he started to latch onto that — Adam West as Batman — as his power source to help him believe he could achieve what he was doing, being from another time, another generation. It occurred to me that Damon and Big Daddy should be two very different kinds of energies. You see it a lot in rock stars, where you meet them in person and they're very fragile and have trouble talking and then they're on stage and they're very powerful and larger than life and you can't believe it's the same person. I think that Damon is a gentle, shy, soft-spoken, bland guy, but when he's Big Daddy he transforms himself, in this pathetic way, to help him get the job done.

This spread: Omari Hardwick plays Marcus, who discovers his ex-cop partner's new identity...

INT. MINDY AND DAMON'S APARTMENT. DAY.

There's nobody here. Suddenly, the LOCK on the door flies out and onto the floor. Sergeant Marcus walks in.

He inspects the apartment, stopping at the wall. He studies the pyramid of comic-book style portraits. The lower ones - all the gangsters Damon and Mindy have killed, including Rasul - have red crosses through them. Marcus's gaze moves to the top of the pyramid and lingers on the picture of Frank.

Marcus moves on, notes the huge stash of weapons. He opens drawers and rifles through their contents. He picks up what appears to be a home-made COMIC, and begins to read...

YC COPS LEA
VAR ON DRUGS

MARK MILLAR ON...

THE CREATION OF BIG DADDY

My idea originally was that Big Daddy wasn't the cop he says he was, he was just another loser, because I thought it was sadder to have that twist as well — that it was just a guy, an accountant, selling his comic collection to buy stuff to fight crime. Matthew felt that was too creepy for the movie though. Originally I was going to make it almost exactly like the movie in the comic, but I changed it back, because whenever I tell friends that aren't comic people, they say, "Oh, no, I prefer him just being the cop, he shouldn't be the loser," but the comic fans tend to prefer it having that extra twist, because otherwise, if he's a revenge cop, he's just Frank Castle. I think that comic guys have seen that a lot, whereas movie guys haven't. Giving it that extra twist makes it more interesting to a comic book audience, and primarily with my comic obviously that's who I'm appealing to, I don't really care about the movie audience.

JANE GOLDMAN ON...

BIG DADDY'S MOVIE BACKSTORY

There needed to be a common enemy that tied all the characters together for the sake of telling the story in a cinematic way, and so it made sense for Big Daddy to have a past that could have tied him in with Frank while still being a good guy. So the cop storyline suggested itself very readily.

The idea is that Big Daddy is an inherently good guy, he was a cop, and we feel he was a cop because he genuinely felt that that was the right thing to do, he wanted to fight crime. He's also a comic book fan, he has that in common with Dave. But his life went absolutely tragically wrong when he was offered the opportunity to be on the payroll of the bad guys, the organized crime guys. He turned it down and as a result was completely turned over by them and had personal tragedy that led from that, and was put in prison and his wife died. He's basically been through hell, he's missed the first few years of his daughter's childhood, his life has absolutely been torn apart, so when he comes out he's a man with a serious vendetta. He's also slightly lost it and is descending deeper and deeper into madness as his desire for revenge grows. It's a plan that's been many years brewing, but he's decided to train his daughter as a little killing machine, to train her up as an assassin so the two of them can go out and fight crime as a crime-fighting duo. Partly it's his love of comic books that's made him bring that element in and partly it's been to make it fun for her, to make it palatable for a little girl.

This spread and following two spreads: Romita drew a cover and several pages for the scene in which Marcus picks up Damon's home-made comic, and learns the backstory of Big Daddy and Hit-Girl.

METRO EDITION
YC COPS LEA
VAR ON DRUGS

NYPD

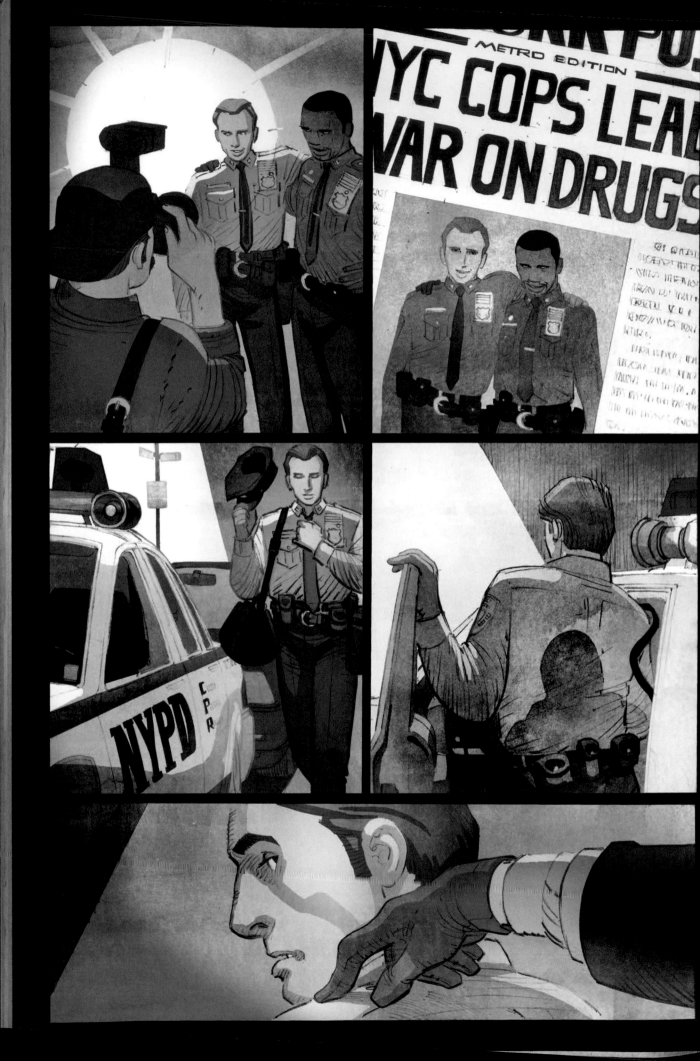

CATESSEN
MACREADY

BD
HG

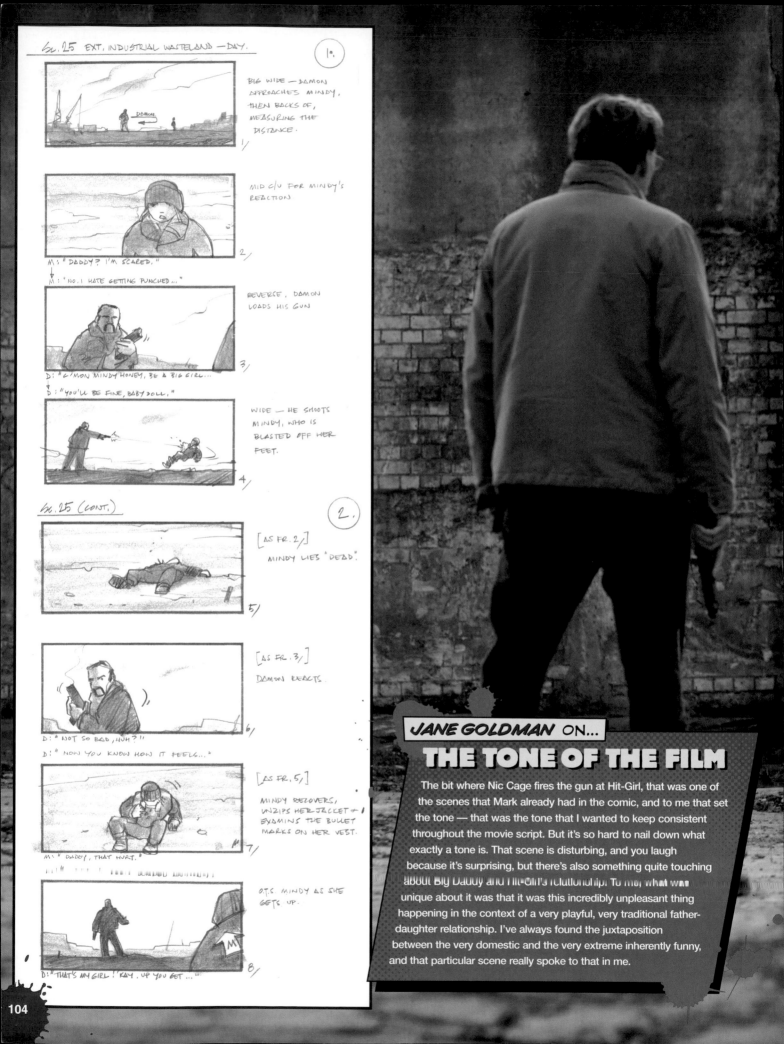

SC. 25 EXT. INDUSTRIAL WASTELAND — DAY.

1.

BIG WIDE — DAMON APPROACHES MINDY, THEN BACKS OF, MEASURING THE DISTANCE.

1/

MID C/U FOR MINDY'S REACTION

2/

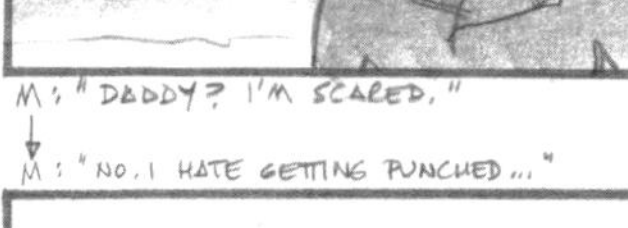

M: "DADDY? I'M SCARED."

M: "NO. I HATE GETTING PUNCHED..."

REVERSE. DAMON LOADS HIS GUN

3/

D: "C'MON MINDY HONEY, BE A BIG GIRL...

D: "YOU'LL BE FINE, BABY DOLL."

WIDE — HE SHOOTS MINDY, WHO IS BLASTED OFF HER FEET.

4/

SC. 25 (CONT.)

2.

[AS FR. 2/]

MINDY LIES "DEAD".

5/

[AS FR. 3/]

DAMON REACTS.

6/

D: "NOT SO BAD, HUH?"

D: "NOW YOU KNOW HOW IT FEELS..."

[AS FR. 5/]

MINDY RECOVERS, UNZIPS HER JACKET & EXAMINS THE BULLET MARKS ON HER VEST.

7/

M: "DADDY, THAT HURT."

O.T.S. MINDY AS SHE GETS UP.

8/

D: "THAT'S MY GIRL! KAY. UP YOU GET..."

JANE GOLDMAN ON...
THE TONE OF THE FILM

The bit where Nic Cage fires the gun at Hit-Girl, that was one of the scenes that Mark already had in the comic, and to me that set the tone — that was the tone that I wanted to keep consistent throughout the movie script. But it's so hard to nail down what exactly a tone is. That scene is disturbing, and you laugh because it's surprising, but there's also something quite touching about Big Daddy and Hit-Girl's relationship. To me, what was unique about it was that it was this incredibly unpleasant thing happening in the context of a very playful, very traditional father-daughter relationship. I've always found the juxtaposition between the very domestic and the very extreme inherently funny, and that particular scene really spoke to that in me.

MARK MILLAR ON...

DAMON SHOOTS MINDY

That was the very first scene I wrote in the comic — it was originally the opening to issue one — and it was the first scene they filmed as well. It was really bizarre.

I remember the first day of filming was in a sewage factory in London. I didn't even know these places existed — you flush the toilet and don't really think about it after that... I didn't realize it's all pooled, it's like a reservoir of excrement, actually *six* reservoirs of excrement over a gigantic area in the East End of London. It's the most disgusting place I've ever been in my life! The air, the minute you get out of the car, smells of sewage for a mile around. We were there for two days, and by the end of each day your clothes smell of sewage; even after three or four washes, your hair smells. It's horrible. And that's where we shot that scene, where Nic's shooting Chloë. It's funny because that was my favorite scene. There were a few drawings I did to begin with, before I started writing, there was Kick-Ass getting shot by gangsters, and another one was a father shooting at his daughter who's wearing a bulletproof vest so that she overcomes her fear of bullets and guns, that's just part of her training. You flinch when you're watching it though, the way she goes down is so severe.

DAMON (CONT'D)
Handgun bullet goes more than 700 miles an hour, so at close range like this, the force is gonna take you right off your feet, for sure. But it's really no more painful than a punch in the chest. Okay?

MINDY
No. I hate getting punched in the chest.

DAMON
You'll be fine, baby doll.

Before she can protest, he releases the slide, takes the safety off, aims the gun at her and fires off a round.

We pull back to see that the car is inside a CRUSHER. Mindy smiles and hits a BUTTON. The crusher grinds into action. Momentarily, a small metal CUBE lands at her feet.

MINDY
What a douche.

MATTHEW VAUGHN ON...

THE US RATINGS SYSTEM

I don't quite understand the ratings system in America. Apparently, I can say to you, "I'm going to fuck you up bad tonight!" and you'll get a PG-13, but if I say, "I wanna fuck you bad tonight!" you get an R. I was scratching my head at that one when I found that out.

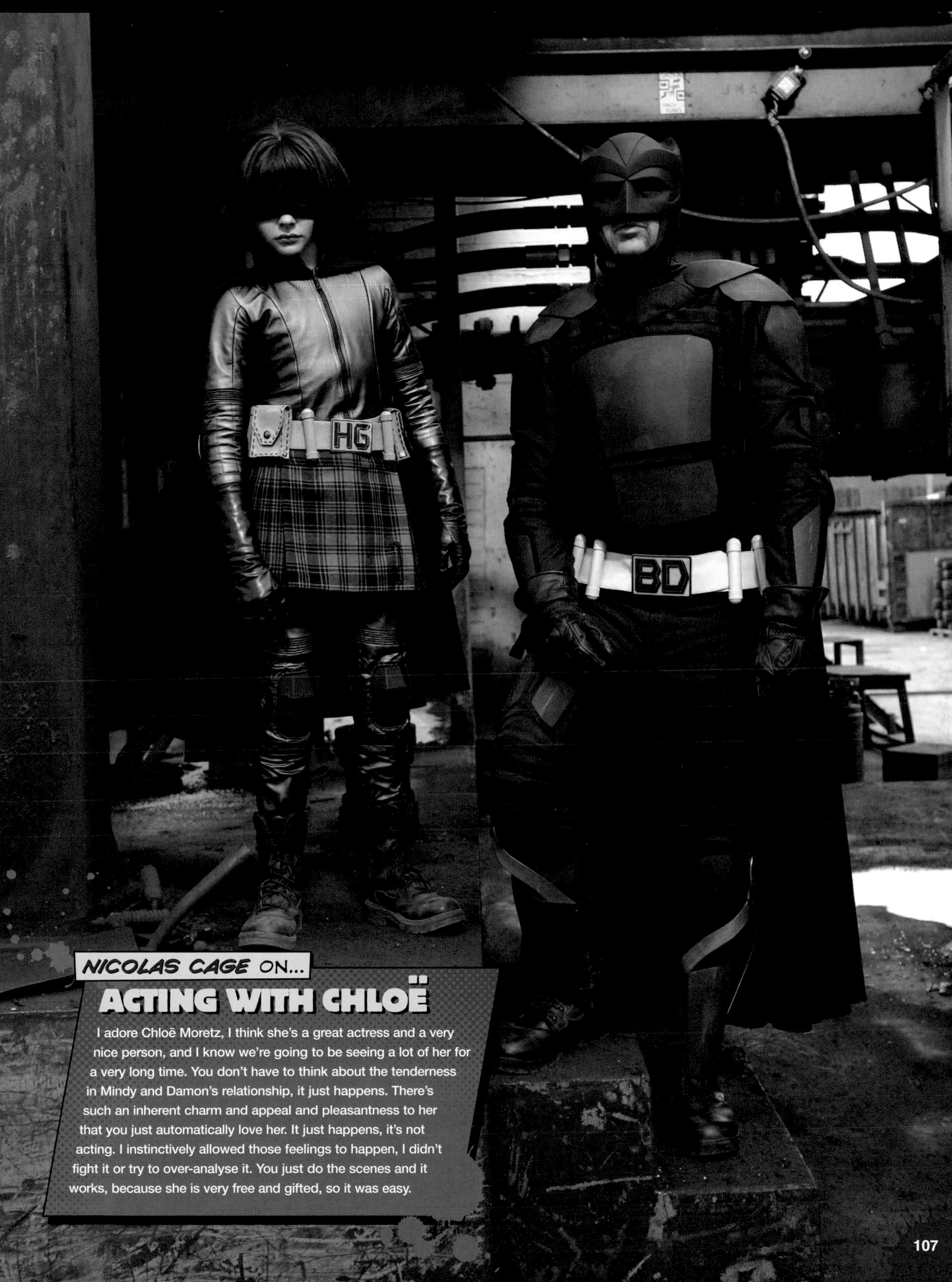

NICOLAS CAGE ON...

ACTING WITH CHLOË

I adore Chloë Moretz, I think she's a great actress and a very nice person, and I know we're going to be seeing a lot of her for a very long time. You don't have to think about the tenderness in Mindy and Damon's relationship, it just happens. There's such an inherent charm and appeal and pleasantness to her that you just automatically love her. It just happens, it's not acting. I instinctively allowed those feelings to happen, I didn't fight it or try to over-analyse it. You just do the scenes and it works, because she is very free and gifted, so it was easy.

MARK MILLAR ON...

THE APARTMENT

The set that really got to me was the home of Big Daddy and Hit-Girl, because it was exactly the way I had it in my head — they had guns all over the walls, and pin ups of all the guys they were going to kill and everything. That was like a panel coming to life, seeing it in three dimensions and walking round, looking round and seeing it from different angles. Then seeing somebody who's a big-name actor like Nicolas Cage sitting in those surroundings talking to this other little character you made up... that was the biggest shock for me.

JANE GOLDMAN ON…

HIT-GIRL AND SWEARING

Maybe it's being a writer or maybe it's just the way I am — I've always felt people overreact appallingly to [bad] language. They're just words, just letters in a different order. I do appreciate that some people are offended by them, but the beautiful thing about cinema is that it's not in your face, you choose to go and see a movie and you generally have a good idea of what kind of movie it is, so I don't think it's going to offend anyone who's chosen to go and see the movie if it is in there. I'm always startled that people seem to be more offended by the use of language than by violence. That absolutely amazes me, it just seems to be such misplaced outrage. If people are startled by the fact that Hit-Girl's being violent in the movie, that's something they're entitled to feel, but the fact that they would probably be *more* startled by the fact that she says "cunt"… I think it makes sense in the context of the character.

What's really interesting is that Big Daddy *doesn't* swear, he's kind of a gentleman, but you get the feeling that as part of her education he has shown her all sorts of movies — John Woo movies or other violent movies or action movies — so that's the world she's grown up in, that's her world. You sense that's where the swearing comes from with her — she's not mixed with other kids. It works in the context of the character, it's not just us saying, "I think it's funny if kids swear." I don't think that's the reason why Mark did it and I don't think that's the reason why we've done it. But I don't have a moral issue with children swearing.

INT. MINDY AND DAMON'S APARTMENT. DAY.
A veritable arsenal of WEAPONS are spread out all over the room. Damon is inking at his drawing board again. Behind him, the pyramid of comicbook-style portraits is now complete.

MARK MILLAR ON...

THE WALL

Nic Cage's character is a comic fan, and all the drawings he does — about fifty portraits of all the gangsters he's going to kill — every one of them was drawn by Johnny and then painted by Dean White, the book's colorist.

This spread: A selection of production art created for Damon and Mindy's villains wall and based upon John Romita Jr.'s vision (left).

JOHN ROMITA JR. ON...

THE VILLAINS WALL

They wanted fifty or sixty gangster mug-shots, and since there are only half a dozen to a dozen actors playing the gangsters in the film, they needed other faces, so they sent me photos of the production crew, the cameramen and the grips to use. That still only came out to about another twenty guys though, so I still had to create a couple of dozen myself. Then when I was able to go on set at the studio, the backlot, I met the people whose faces they'd sent me to turn into villains and they all got a real kick out of it.

People ask if I put myself in there. I didn't put myself in, and I didn't put Mark in. I don't think there's a way of thug-izing Mark. He's got a baby-face, he can't be turned into a thug. I don't think it's possible.

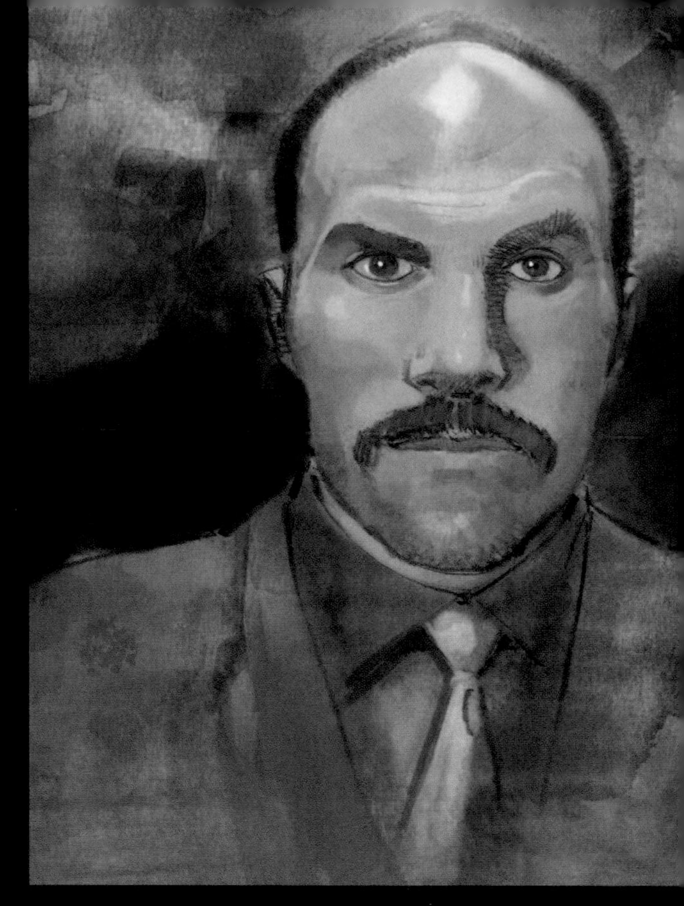

But this is the reality of the situation. This is what happens when you mess with bad people.

MARK MILLAR ON...

CASTING FRANK

British people might remember Mark Strong in *Our Friends in the North*, which is where I first saw him. I watched that again recently for the first time in over ten years, and I was quite shocked to see him being so charming, playing such a likeable character, because he has played a baddie in everything I've seen him in for the last five years. He makes a great baddie because he does have that sinister, Mediterranean look, but he's such a nice person, he's so likeable.

At the time we were initially discussing casting, we were talking about possibly having Jack Nicholson, we were talking about Robert De Niro, there were a whole bunch of people we were thinking about. I was desperate to see who it was going to be because I knew the conclusion was going to be that character doing kung-fu against an eleven-year-old girl. So I can't wait to see Mark Strong on screen fighting a little girl at the end. I wonder what all his thespian mates will make of it!

TRE FERNANDEZ, 30, unlikely to join his local neighbourhood watch scheme any time soon, is here tied to a chair. Tre's fingers are in a pair of heavy-duty BOLT-CUTTERS held by CODY, 40 and shifty-looking.

Several other goons surround them - let's call them GINGER, SCARY, SPORTY, BABY and POSH. And here's FRANK D'AMICO, 50s and his right-hand man, BIG JOE. You know by the cut of Frank's suit that he's in charge.

JANE GOLDMAN ON...

FRANK AT HOME

I've always found the juxtaposition between the very domestic and the very extreme inherently funny. The thing that we've tried to do with Red Mist and his father is again to bring out that contrast. These are people who do dreadful things, but they have moments of domesticity where they're discussing incredibly banal things, or you see them in a home setting. That to me is both funny and interesting. A lot of the time, when you see villains or you see unpleasant things happening in films, they're very much in their villain's lair, so the idea of seeing them in a domestic setting amuses me because of that. There was a British TV comedy show called *Big Train*, which had a recurring sketch which featured a sort of Ming the Merciless character, with the space emperor costume, and his advisor. The sketches were acted very naturalistically and they were always talking about very banal stuff and you'd occasionally see him hoovering or answering his phone, "Hello?" I loved that, that juxtaposition always made me laugh. It was that sort of tone that struck me about *Kick-Ass* and that I wanted to run with.

PRODUCTION DESIGNER
RUSSELL DE ROZARIO ON...

FRANK'S APARTMENT SET

There's shorthand in Frank's apartment to tell you about what Frank's world is, and from the sum total of all those parts you can work out he's obviously really powerful and rich. He can afford to build an apartment on top of a skyscraper, that's his thing. He's bought this picture-book vista to look at in the morning, and he has millions of dollars' worth of art hanging on his walls. And that is the product of his criminal empire.

We looked at pictures of megalomaniacs' houses. They've all got pictures of themselves all over the place — even minor megalomaniacs tend to have a lot of pictures of themselves shaking hands with some Queen or some head of state or whatever — and they tend to collect things that are an ostentatious display of their wealth. I suppose they're investments as well, but having your own personal art gallery, like a room out of the Tate Gallery, as your lobby does really tell everybody, "Look, I'm worth a lot more than you. Fuck off."

Above: Evidence of what Vic Gigante (played by Xander Berkeley) got up to down in Tijuana last year...

GIGANTE

Listen: The cops pay me to nail the bad guys. You pay me not to. Everything else is a grey area. There's no evidence on Kickass, and trust me, folks here ain't in a hurry to find any. He's just doing what a lot of 'em would like to do.

FRANK

Fuck you very much, Vic. Just do it, okay?

GIGANTE

Frankie -

Frank picks up a framed photo on his desk. We can't see it.

FRANK

Boy, you sure look good in that picture I have of you down in Tijuana last year. Maybe I should put it on Facebook. You think?

JOHN ROMITA JR. ON...

HIS CAMEO

Visiting the movie set completely turned me into a child again. Myself and my family were on set for about five days. The majority of the time they were shooting the scenes in the comic book store coffee shop. Actually, I was given a moment to get into a scene as an extra, and my son also. I'm a barista behind the counter, and I actually turn the sound up on a television behind the counter in the comic book store when the actors ask me to. They managed to reduce the size of my nose on my shots so that it's not too out of whack! I had no dialogue. I don't think they wanted to ruin the film that much. Then my son was an extra going through the comic racks as Chris is being approached by the other kids. It's a great drinking story — my part expands the more alcohol I ingest. It was more fun than you can imagine, and anybody that goes through a similar situation would probably say the same thing — you giggle like a child. Watching my son's eyes light up and hearing him tell his friends about it when he got home was worth it in itself.

Top: John Romita Jr. kicks ass on set. *Right*: Romita's son Vinnie also cameos.

A teenage boy climbs out - CHRIS D'AMICO, 17 and self-conscious. He shuffles in, shadowed by a HUGE GOON.

Chris begins to browse a rack of comics, sneaking a look over at Dave and his friends before looking hurriedly away.

DAVE
Is it just me, or do you feel kinda sorry for Chris D'Amico?

I FIND A LIL'
ZOOT TAKES
THE EDGE
OFF WHEN I'M
ON PATROL

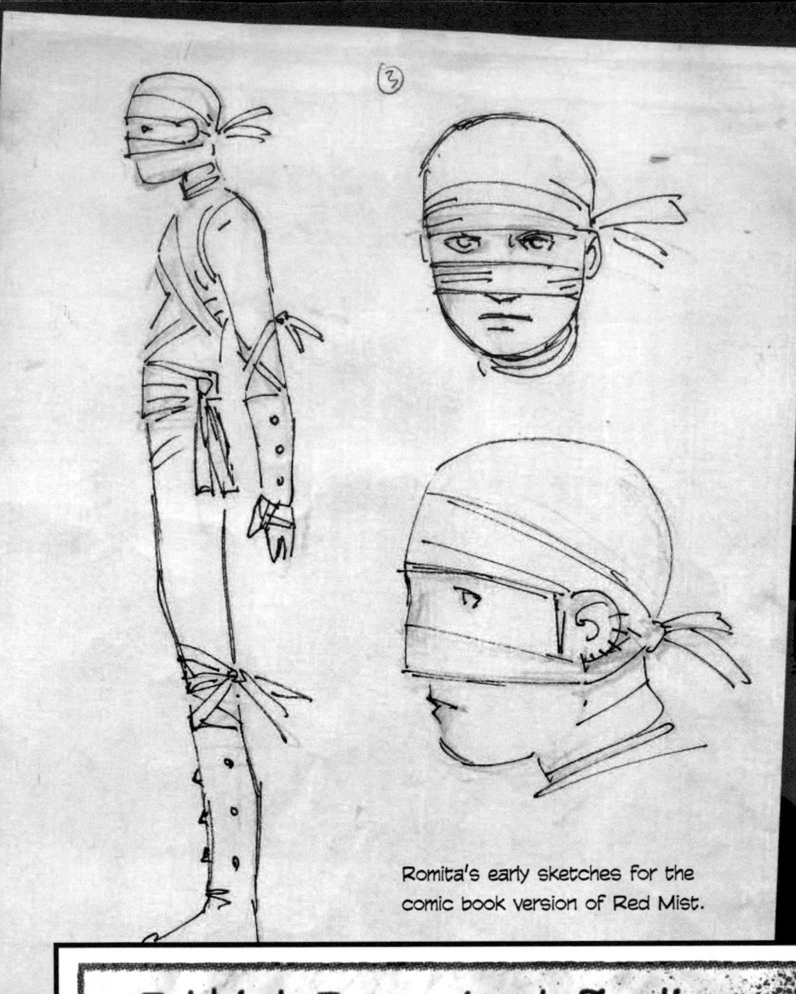

Romita's early sketches for the comic book version of Red Mist.

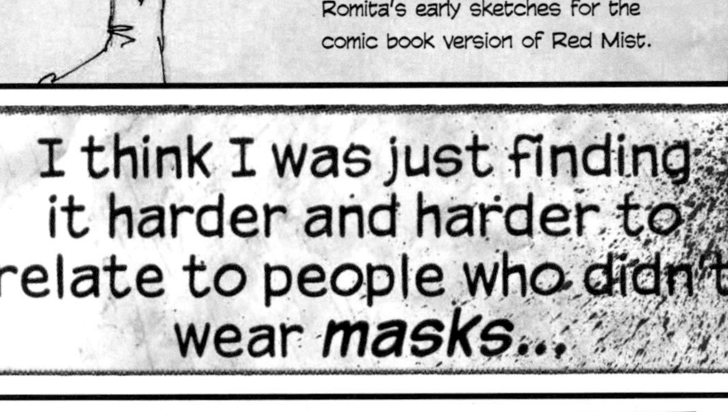

I think I was just finding it harder and harder to relate to people who didn't wear *masks...*

MARK MILLAR ON...

RED MIST

The biggest change to my original comic book plot was that I was going to have Red Mist as a hit-man who was brought in by the gangsters to take out these superheroes that were emerging, so he was just a guy that was a brilliant hit-man who realized, "Look, the only way you can get these geeks is to dress up like them and get their trust, and then come in and start killing them." But Matthew wanted to do a Harry Osborn and Norman Osborn father and son thing, and we talked about it and he talked me round, so we made Red Mist the son of the gangster. So that was an idea that we took from the movie and incorporated into the comic. It didn't really mean much re-writing or anything in the comic, it just meant a couple of subtle changes, but that's quite a big dynamic that's different because of the movie.

Red Mist is based on the idea of wanting to show a superhero that you had never really seen before, a guy that's having sex with his groupies, smoking dope in his car and all that kind of thing; you never really see superheroes doing what kids about that age do. So Dave is the geeky version of what a kid like that would do as a superhero, Red Mist is the cooler version, because he's got the car and the girls and all that stuff.

JANE GOLDMAN ON...

RED MIST

The idea of Red Mist and his relationship with his father was something that we wanted to explore that wasn't there initially. The idea of him being motivated by wanting to be accepted by his father and wanting to be in the family business, but maybe in some sense being a disappointment to his father, that kind of father-son relationship interested me, so that was something which evolved.

For the first six weeks we always referred to Chris Mintz-Plasse as McLovin', which I felt so bad about. Talking to each other we would say, "We've got McLovin' coming in for a photo shoot at eleven o'clock," and it's terrible because he's such a good actor and such a nice person, but he made such an impact with his first role that you can only think of him as McLovin' until you really get to know him. I love the idea that he's about to play another iconic character now though, and I think this'll help move him on from the McLovin' thing. It's a great thing to be a victim of your own success, I suppose, in that regard.

Chris had auditioned for Dave, but just didn't seem quite right. Everybody really liked him and his audition was really funny, but we were worried about Dave being *too* funny, because it might seem like a comedy then. Then we realized that having Chris play a support character like Red Mist brought the whole thing to life. Dave really has to be quite normal — again, it's the Luke Skywalker thing — and then you surround him with cartoon characters, which keeps him going through the movie. Everybody you meet is seen through Dave's eyes. Chris ad-libs quite a lot of his lines and it's absolutely hysterical. There are so many people who could potentially steal the movie, and he's one of them. We loved him so much that we actually beefed up his role in the sequel, he's going to be a really major force in the sequel. That wouldn't have happened unless it was somebody like Chris playing the part.

CHRISTOPHER MINTZ-PLASSE ON...

RED MIST'S LOOK

Chris D'Amico knows so much about comic books. Every time you see him, in every scene, he's always reading, there's always a pile somewhere. He just knows so much about it that I guess, in his mind, Red Mist is who his superhero would be, that's what it would look like, and he'd have that Asian rock star hair — down at the front, up at the back — and that tight leather suit and the fake abs, which he obviously doesn't have, which *I* obviously don't have! It's no Wolverine or Spider-Man or anything, but it's what a seventeen-year-old kid would want to look like as a superhero.

JANE GOLDMAN ON...

CHRISTOPHER MINTZ-PLASSE

Chris has got such a distinctive delivery that once he was on board and those scenes were being rewritten or added to, or new scenes were being written, it was the most fun. Obviously, it's great fun writing for someone specifically, because it's a different process — you hear the actor's voice as well as the voice of the character. And it's particularly fun writing for Chris because his delivery is so distinctive that you can really hear it in your head. It's very gratifying to write dialogue for someone who you know is going to bring an extra layer to it.

Matthew saw the potential in Chris beyond his role in *Superbad* too. And to me it makes perfect sense because, as a person, he's actually *so* far removed from McLovin' — couldn't be more different — and is probably far more similar to Red Mist, although he doesn't have a nasty streak! Chris is not in the least bit geeky, not really interested in anything geeky, doesn't play computer games, is really good at sport, really competitive, is amazing at basketball, amazing at bowling, he's a real guy's guy. He's absolutely not what people expect him to be.

SAMMY SHELDON ON...

RED MIST'S MOVIE COSTUME

For Red Mist, we came up with his costume for the movie, because at that time only the first few comics issues were out and he doesn't appear in those. I linked his costume to his car and the fact that he's a rich boy and he wants to have the coolest of the cool. I used the car as a starting reference, as they wanted that particular car, so there had to be red in there. The original design I did was more red with a little bit of black in, but when we started fitting Chris, he has a very slim figure and the red didn't work quite so well on him. So we reversed everything, which actually gives Red Mist a slightly Gothic feel, which lent itself to his character, which is quite dark — he's not your typical American kid. Because we used the car as a starting point, we thought we'd go with the biker boots, and mirrored that in the elements on his arm.

For Red Mist's head gear, there are certain practical considerations about filming you have to keep in mind, like if you cover the bottom half of someone's face you immediately have a problem with sound and you can't clearly see who it is behind that mask, so we needed to reveal parts of Chris's face in order for it to be recognizable as his alter-ego. We actually ended up drawing on his face in the fitting. I think the end result is kind of cool.

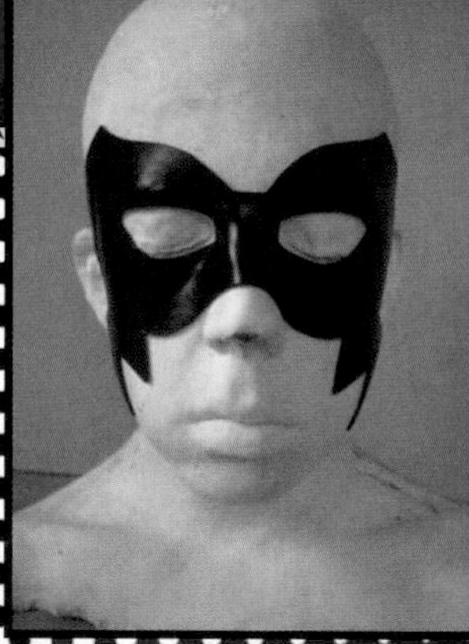

RED MIST'S COSTUME

That came entirely from the designer, Sammy Sheldon — she drew up a picture of him and wanted him to look like the sort of guy that teen manga fans would have a crush on. So he ended up with quite a different look from what we originally had in mind. I saw him as more of a generic superhero-y kind of guy, like somebody that Kick-Ass wishes he could be, a little bit more Batman-y in that kind of sense, but they went for something that would probably work better as a doll or something, which turned out great. I'll trust the designer, in terms of design, more than I'll trust myself, so I went with it.

JOHN ROMITA JR. ON...

RED MIST'S COMIC COSTUME

I went my own way with Red Mist, but, again, I tried to stick with the flavor that Mark and Matthew had asked for. I threw in some gloves and some boots that would be a little bit different. Mark said, "Give it a superhero flair because this kid's got a lot of money," and I went from there. I tried throwing straps around elbows and wrists — something that, while it would look a little bit more expensive, would still be relatively cool-looking — and then we came to the happy medium that we got with the comic. Then I designed the 'M' logo on the chest. It was a confluence of events, a back and forth between Mark and myself, a couple of sketches here and then some agreement. And, of course, other than the chest logo, it looks nothing like what the costume looks like for the movie, and that's fine. Let's have this disparity, I have no problem with it.

LYNDSY FONSECA ON…

CHRISTOPHER MINTZ-PLASSE

Chris is amazing. I saw *Superbad* and I loved it and I knew he was in this movie, but I had no idea what he was going to be like. Then I met him and he's so much fun, we have such a blast. But he is so huge, I had no idea. We'd go out and girls stop him everywhere. Just last night I had to pretend I was his girlfriend to get these chicks to leave him alone. I was like, "Come on honey." People go crazy. They love him.

CHRISTOPHER MINTZ-PLASSE ON...

KICK-ASS

I've read a bunch of comics as my dad is a huge fan and he knows all the Mark Millar stuff. Whenever he goes to the bathroom he's got a pile of comics right there that he reads — he takes thirty-minute craps so he can catch up on all his comics! So I guess when I go to do my business I start reading them as well, as they're right there and it's more entertaining to read something than just sit there on the toilet and daydream!

When I first read the script I thought, "Why the hell are they sending me an action movie?" because I'm this skinny kid who couldn't fight someone for the life of me, and I've done a bunch of comedies and stuff. But the fact that they let me audition for this role, I was really honored. I went and actually auditioned for Kick-Ass, and Matthew said in the audition, "You have too much spunk, too much sass for Kick-Ass," and then right there in the audition told me he wanted me for Chris, which was really awesome.

I'm a huge fan of action movies. How can you not love cars exploding and an eleven-year-old girl killing fifty people and saying "Fucking cunt"? How can you not want to be part of that movie? So that was the main reason I chose it, because I like to do movies that I would want to see in the theater, and I would *definitely* want to see *Kick-Ass* in the theater.

They turn the corner to see: a gorgeous MUSTANG.

DAVE
Sweet!! Is that yours?

CHRIS
Meet the Mist Mobile. Check it out:

He opens the passenger door and Dave gets in.

INT. THE MIST MOBILE/RED MIST ALLEYWAY. NIGHT.

Chris points to various things in the car.

CHRIS
Sat-nav. My iphone - so I can check the website for emergencies while I'm driving around. Uh... Cup holder...

CHRISTOPHER MINTZ-PLASSE ON...

THE MIST MOBILE

I don't know why they trust me with that badass car, man. It's a Mustang GT. The fact that they're trusting me and I've never driven stick... I had to learn to drive that car and then Matthew comes up to me and he's like, "You're gonna do great, and by the way, if you fucking wreck this car you're gonna owe me five hundred grand." I'm like, "Don't put that thought in my mind. Please don't tell me that!" But I drove it once and I hit the clutch and put it in second gear and hit the brakes, so I did well, no crashes.

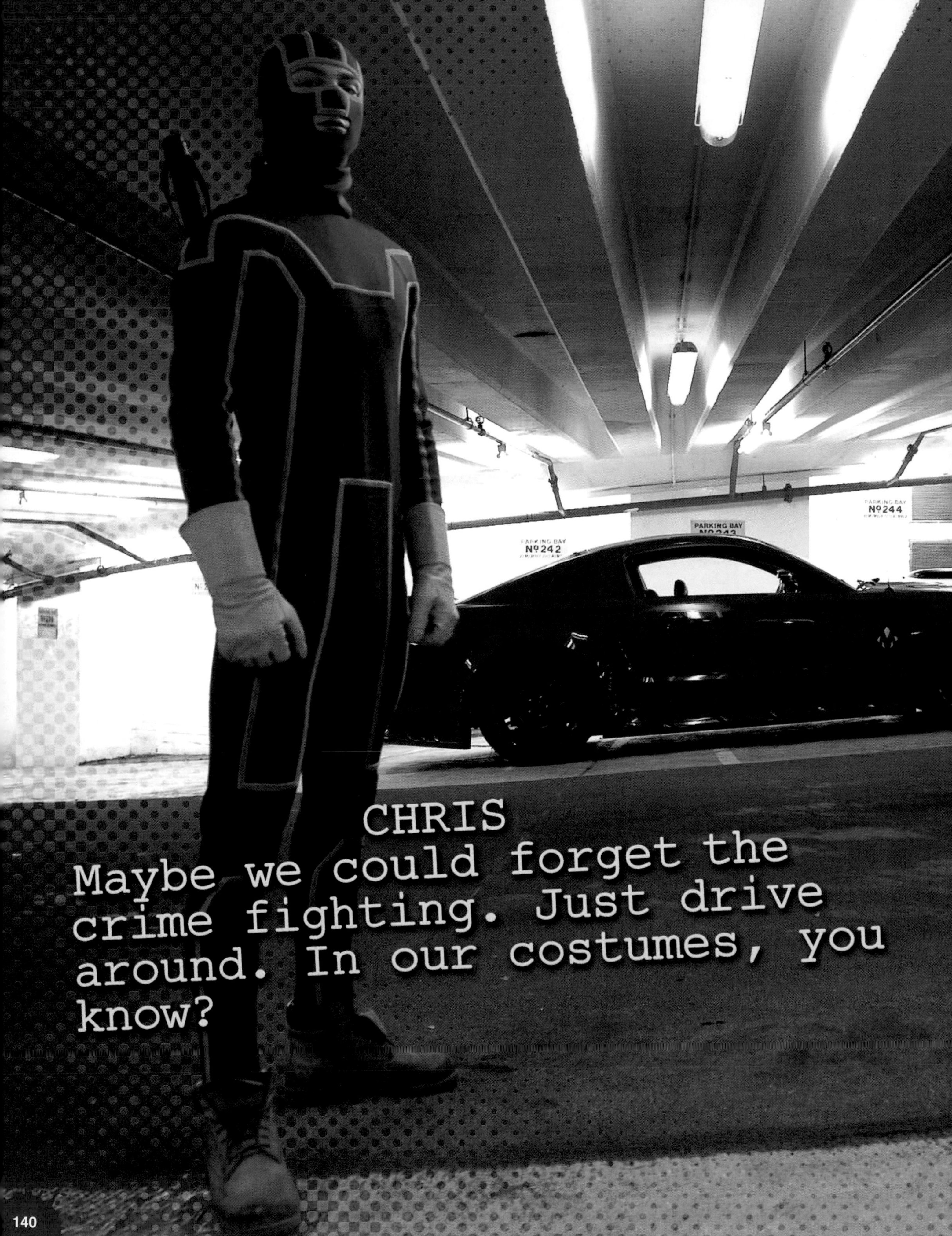
PARKING BAY
Nº244
PARKING BAY
PARKING BAY
Nº242
CHRIS
Maybe we could forget the crime fighting. Just drive around. In our costumes, you know?

SC. 111 INT. (EXT.) MIST MOBILE — NIGHT.

1.

CAMERA TRACKS AFTER CAR.

CAR
1B
CAMERA STOPS TO ALLOW CAR TO EXIT ROUND CORNER.

CAR
2A
PICK UP ROUND THE CORNER AS THE CAR COMES ROUND & DRIVES TO CAMERA.

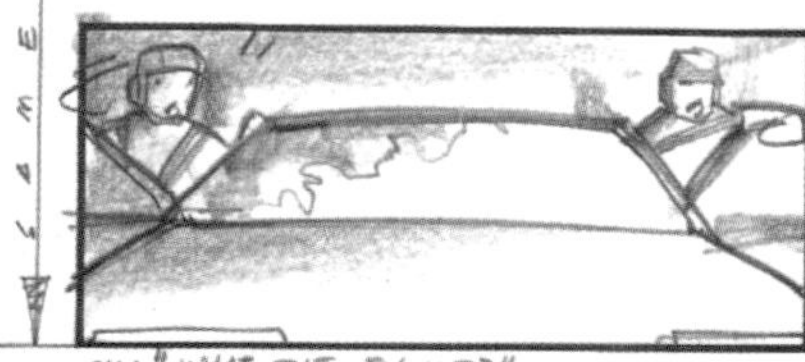

2B
THE CAR PULLS UP JUST INFRONT OF CAMERA. FLAMES ARE REFLECTED IN THE WINDSCREEN. THEY GET OUT.
CH: "WHAT.. THE.. FUCK??"

LUMBER SUPPLIES

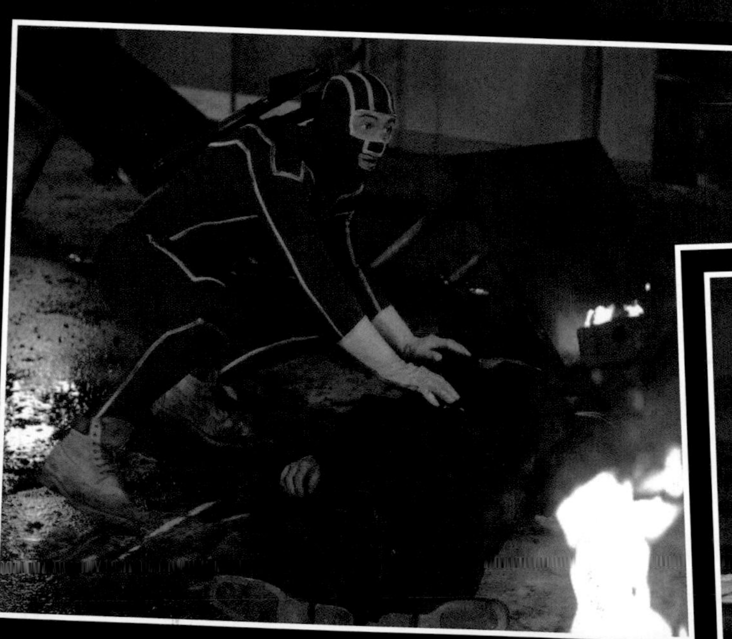

Kick-Ass sets out on patrol with Red Mist, and finds Frank's lumber yard on fire...

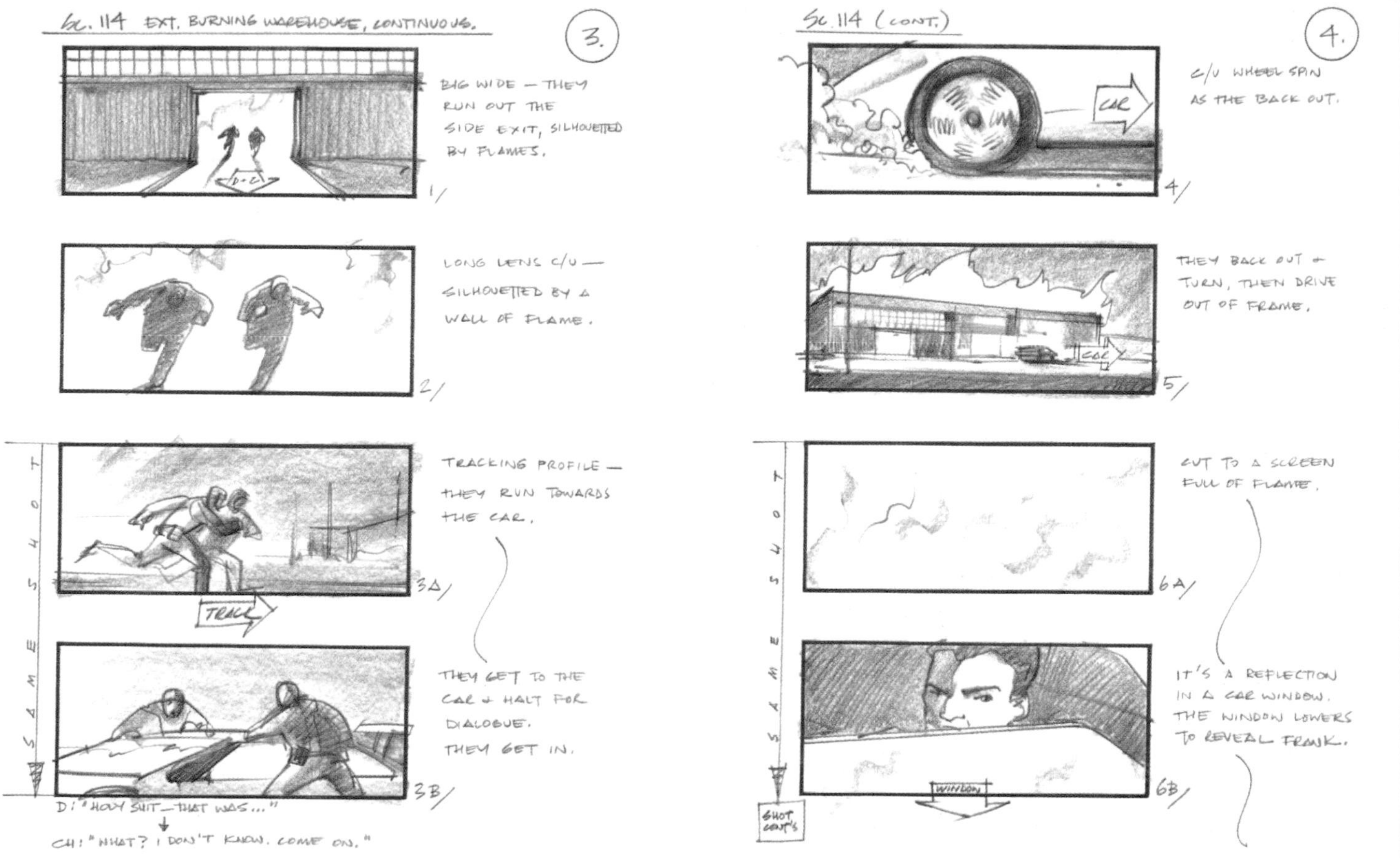

Sc. 114 EXT. BURNING WAREHOUSE, CONTINUOUS. (3.)

BIG WIDE — THEY RUN OUT THE SIDE EXIT, SILHOUETTED BY FLAMES. 1/

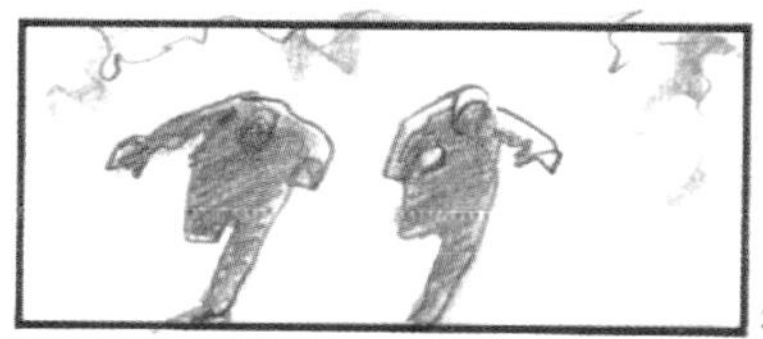

LONG LENS C/U — SILHOUETTED BY A WALL OF FLAME. 2/

TRACKING PROFILE — THEY RUN TOWARDS THE CAR. 3A/

THEY GET TO THE CAR & HALT FOR DIALOGUE. THEY GET IN. 3B/

D: "HOLY SHIT — THAT WAS..."

CH: "WHAT? I DON'T KNOW. COME ON."

SAME SHOT

Sc. 114 (CONT.) (4.)

C/U WHEEL SPIN AS THE BACK OUT. 4/

THEY BACK OUT & TURN, THEN DRIVE OUT OF FRAME. 5/

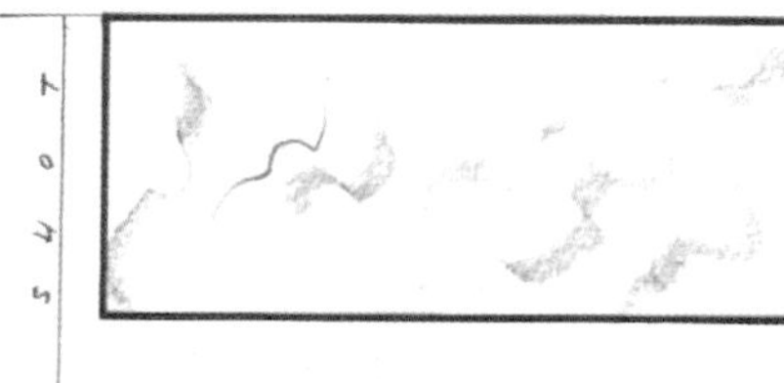

CUT TO A SCREEN FULL OF FLAME. 6A/

IT'S A REFLECTION IN A CAR WINDOW. THE WINDOW LOWERS TO REVEAL FRANK. 6B/

WINDOW

SAME SHOT

SHOT CONT'S

EXT. D'AMICO'S LUMBER YARD. NIGHT.

Dave and Chris emerge from the flames, looking every inch the authentic superheroes, bar the fact that they haven't rescued anyone and Chris appears to be holding A BURNT TEDDY BEAR.

Dave reveals his secret identity to Katie.

KATIE
...Where? What kind of a thing? I thought you were done with that?

We now intercut between Katie and Dave.

DAVE
This is the last time. I totally swear... Well, I wish you <u>wouldn't</u> worry.

KATIE
I can't help it. I <u>do</u>. Because I...
(is she gonna say it?)
...Care about you. A lot.

In the alley, Dave can't control his giant smile.

DAVE
I... care about you a lot, too.

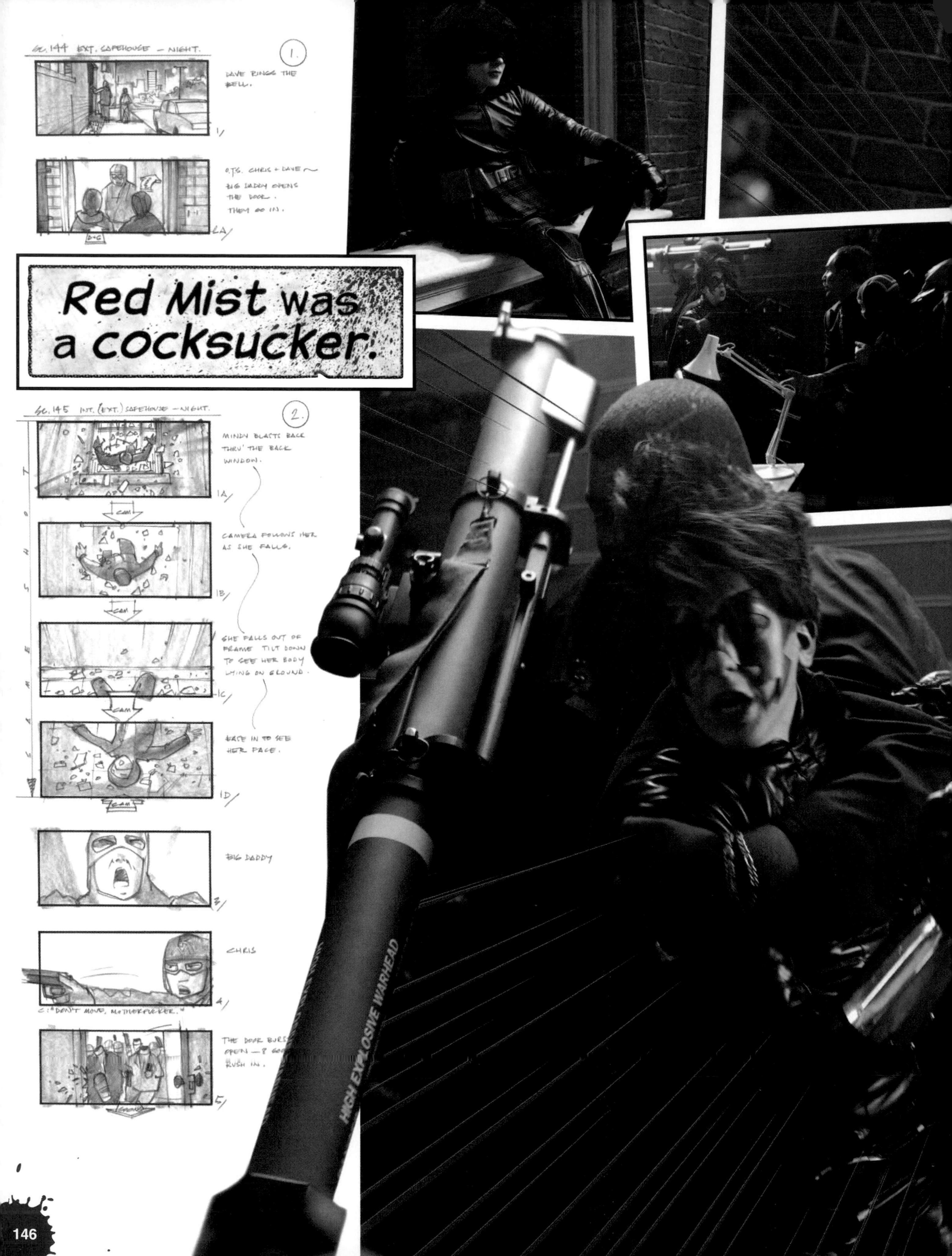
SC. 144 EXT. SAFEHOUSE – NIGHT.
1.
DAVE RINGS THE BELL.
1/
O.T.S. CHRIS + DAVE ~ BIG DADDY OPENS THE DOOR. THEY GO IN.
2A/
Red Mist was a cocksucker.
SC. 145 INT. (EXT.) SAFEHOUSE – NIGHT.
2.
MINDY BLASTS BACK THRU' THE BACK WINDOW.
1A/
CAM
CAMERA FOLLOWS HER AS SHE FALLS.
1B/
CAM
SHE FALLS OUT OF FRAME TILT DOWN TO SEE HER BODY LYING ON GROUND.
1C/
CAM
EASE IN TO SEE HER FACE.
1D/
CAM
BIG DADDY
3/
CHRIS
4/
C: "DON'T MOVE, MOTHERFUCKER."
THE DOOR BURS
OPEN — 8
RUSH IN.
5/
HIGH EXPLOSIVE WARHEAD

Red Mist's true allegiance becomes clear. Kick-Ass and Big Daddy are captured while Hit-Girl is left for dead...

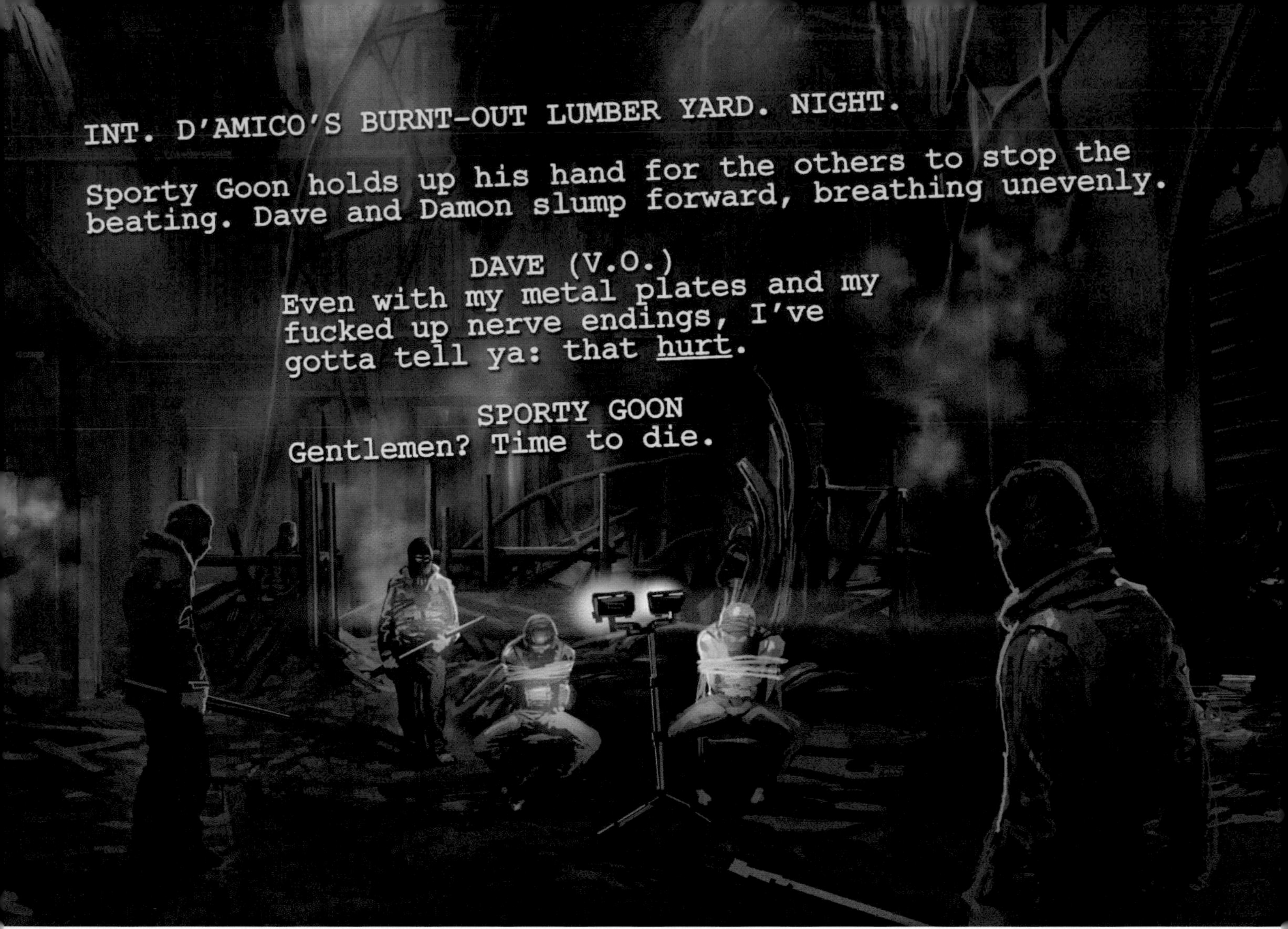

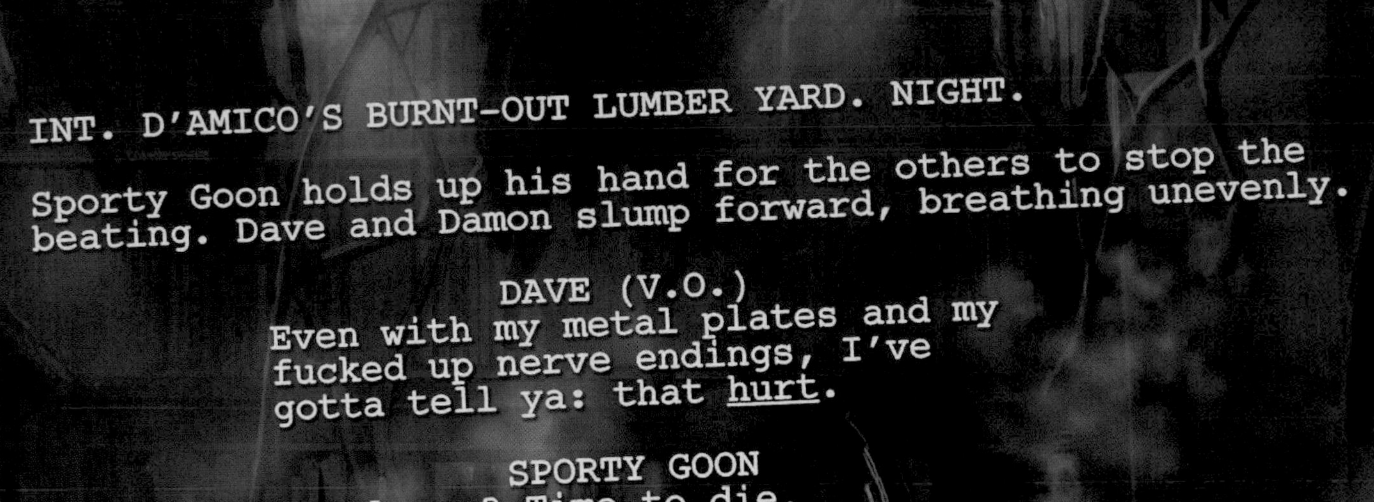

INT. D'AMICO'S BURNT-OUT LUMBER YARD. NIGHT.
Sporty Goon holds up his hand for the others to stop the beating. Dave and Damon slump forward, breathing unevenly.
DAVE (V.O.)
Even with my metal plates and my fucked up nerve endings, I've gotta tell ya: that hurt.
SPORTY GOON
Gentlemen? Time to die.

Big Daddy and Kick-Ass await execution live on the internet, courtesy of Frank's goons.

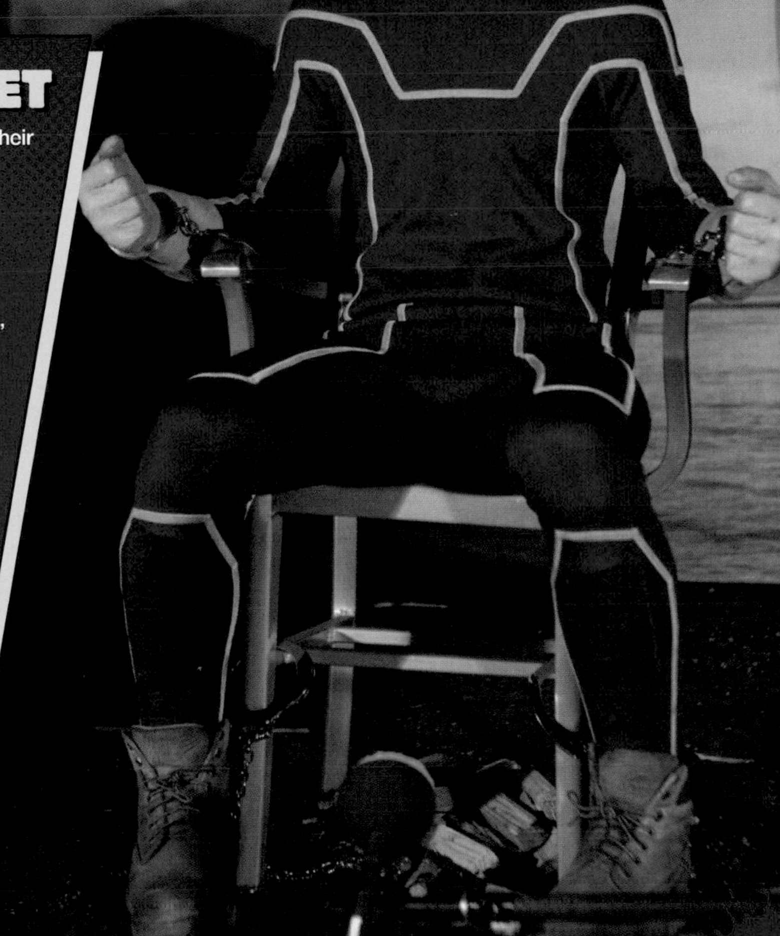

RUSSELL DE ROZARIO ON...

THE WAREHOUSE SET

What's interesting is that people thought it was affecting their health, they were like, "I'm breathing in all this shit and it's horrible."

"Really? What are you breathing in?"

"Well, it's all burnt out."

"But it's all fake, it's not real."

"But it's horrible being in there, after a fire and everything."

"There's been no fire. It's just been built."

"But I've got all black stuff up my nose."

"Well, it's in your imagination because there's very little real ash in there."

Most of it's fake stuff that we've made — fake ash and fake bits of fire and fake beams and everything. And it's really interesting how psychologically it affects them. I built a snow set once, it was in the summer — and people were cold. They were coming in from summer heat outside, and it's a bit colder inside because it's in the shade, but you'd see people in jumpers doing fake shivering. So it's a great sideways compliment really, that they were moaning about breathing in all that imagined toxic crap. Even my guys were feeling sorry for them, saying, "Oh it's terrible for them in there."

"But why? You know even better than they do that it's fake!"

"Oh yeah, I suppose..."

MINDY
Let him go, the whole thing starts up again. New guys. New supplies. All our hard work, wasted.

DAVE
I know, but this plan of yours. Even if there were <u>ten</u> of you -

MINDY
My mom already died for nothing. I'm not gonna let my dad die for nothing too.

DAVE
You can't do this on your own. It's suicide.

MINDY
Exactly. You wanna deal with owing my dad? Then shut the hell up and pick your weapon.

Hit-Girl comes to the rescue, but not in time to save her father — leaving her to finish the mission he started.

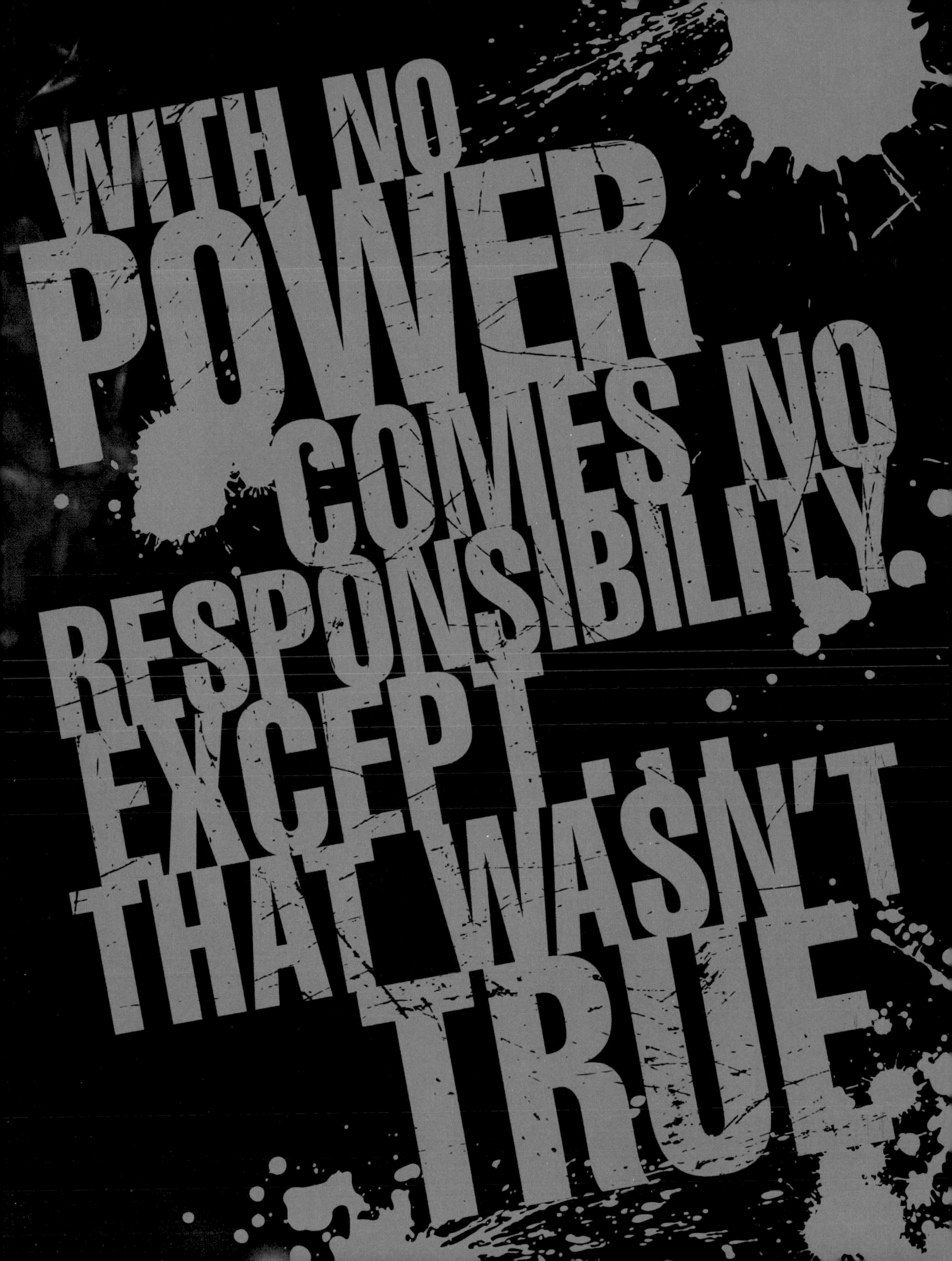
WITH NO
POWER
COMES NO
RESPONSIBILITY.
EXCEPT
THAT WASN'T
TRUE.

Mindy arrives at the lobby of Frank's apartment building...

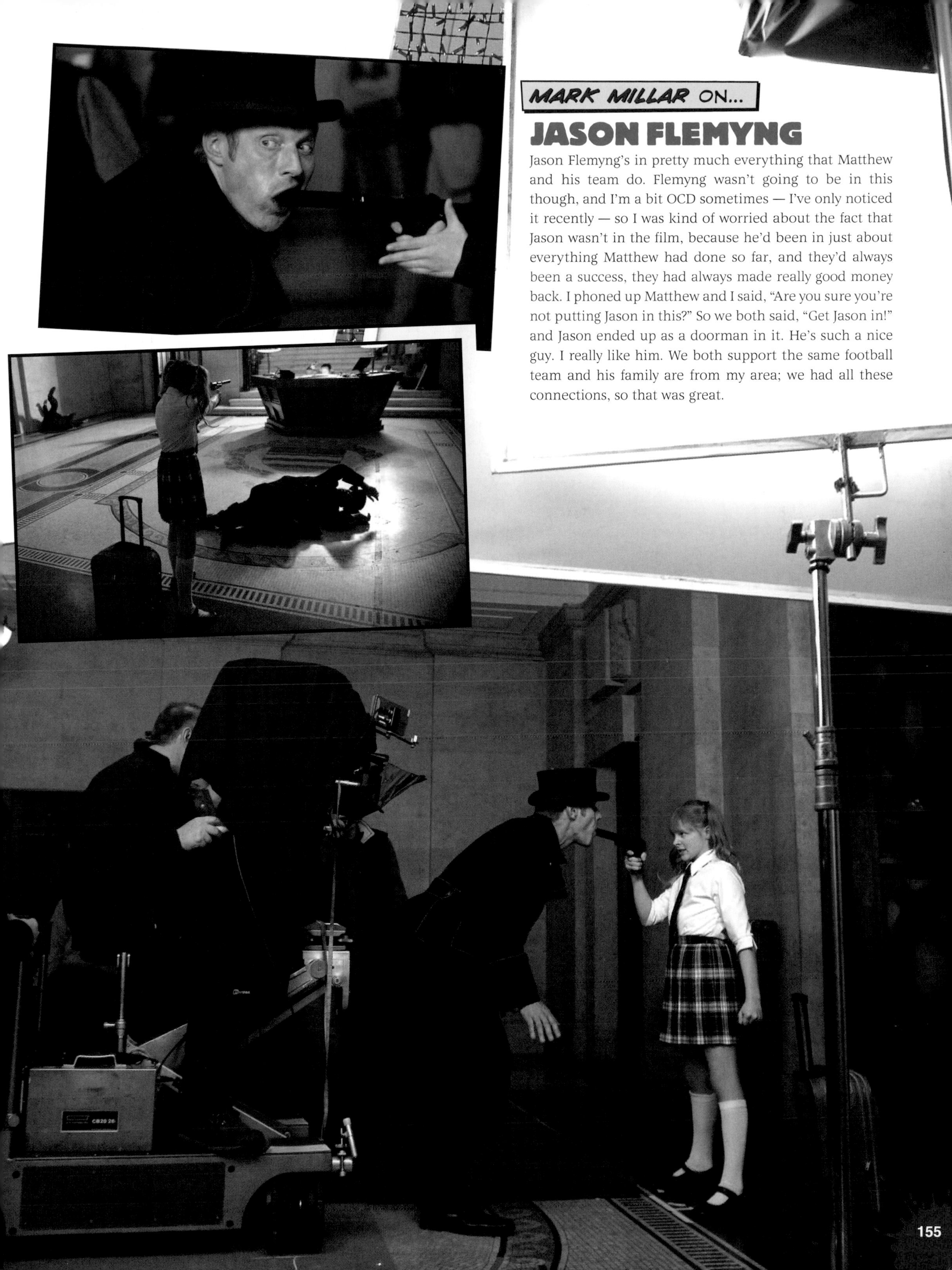

MARK MILLAR ON...

JASON FLEMYNG

Jason Flemyng's in pretty much everything that Matthew and his team do. Flemyng wasn't going to be in this though, and I'm a bit OCD sometimes — I've only noticed it recently — so I was kind of worried about the fact that Jason wasn't in the film, because he'd been in just about everything Matthew had done so far, and they'd always been a success, they had always made really good money back. I phoned up Matthew and I said, "Are you sure you're not putting Jason in this?" So we both said, "Get Jason in!" and Jason ended up as a doorman in it. He's such a nice guy. I really like him. We both support the same football team and his family are from my area; we had all these connections, so that was great.

Cut To:
Mindy uses the 1st guard as a spring board exiting the lift.

Continued:
She slams the 2nd guard on to the table.

Cut To:
She flips over and lands, stabbing him through the heart.

Cut To:
Mindy Pulls a gun and shoots.

MATTHEW VAUGHN ON...

KICK-ASS ACTION

There's nothing in this film that couldn't happen. Some of the action sequences are... you know, we're making a movie, so I pushed the boundaries as far as I could. There are a few moments you'd maybe pull off one in a million times if you were doing it for real, but I tried to ground this as much in reality without it being a documentary.

It hasn't got a serious bone in its body, to be frank. But it ain't a spoof or a comedy either. When I say it's not serious, I mean it's meant to be fun. Someone described it as "Teenage Tarantino". And as much as I'd love to think I could walk on that man's coattails, that's a description that made me smile.

... but when the elevator doors in Frank's penthouse open, it's Hit-Girl who attacks.

MARK MILLAR ON...

THE JETPACK

The thing that was really important to us was that they never, ever use anything you can't buy on eBay. Every single thing that's in the movie in terms of superhero equipment is something you can buy on eBay, right down to the jetpack at the end, which Kick-Ass uses to attack Frank's apartment. I think they cost 150 grand. You can buy a jetpack. We made sure everything was something you could get your hands on, so it doesn't become like *The Dark Knight* where you have Lucius Fox saying, "I've got my new two million dollar thing here that'll help you beat the Joker." If it's not something you can go online and buy, it doesn't make it into the movie.

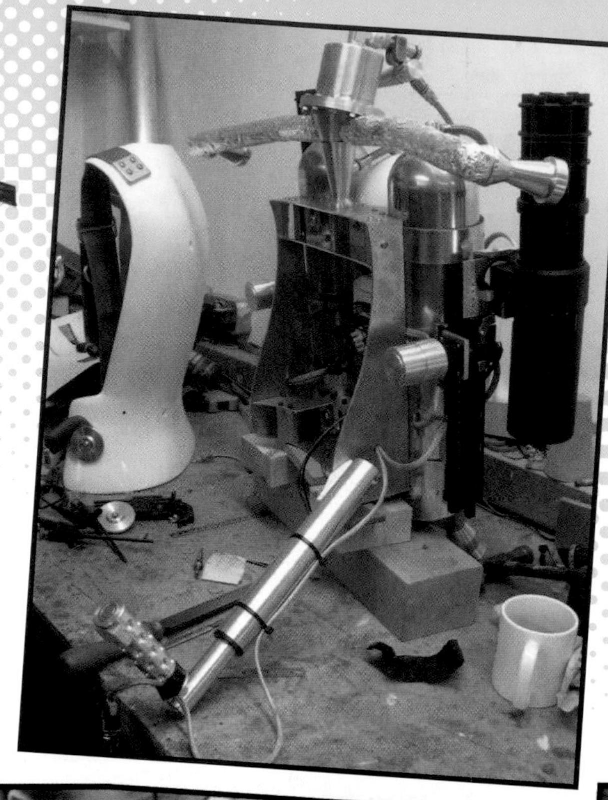

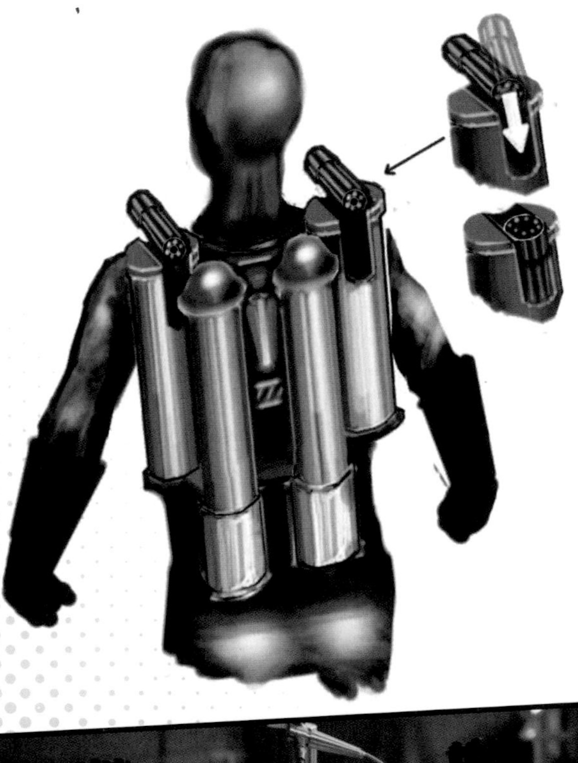

EXT D'AMICO APART

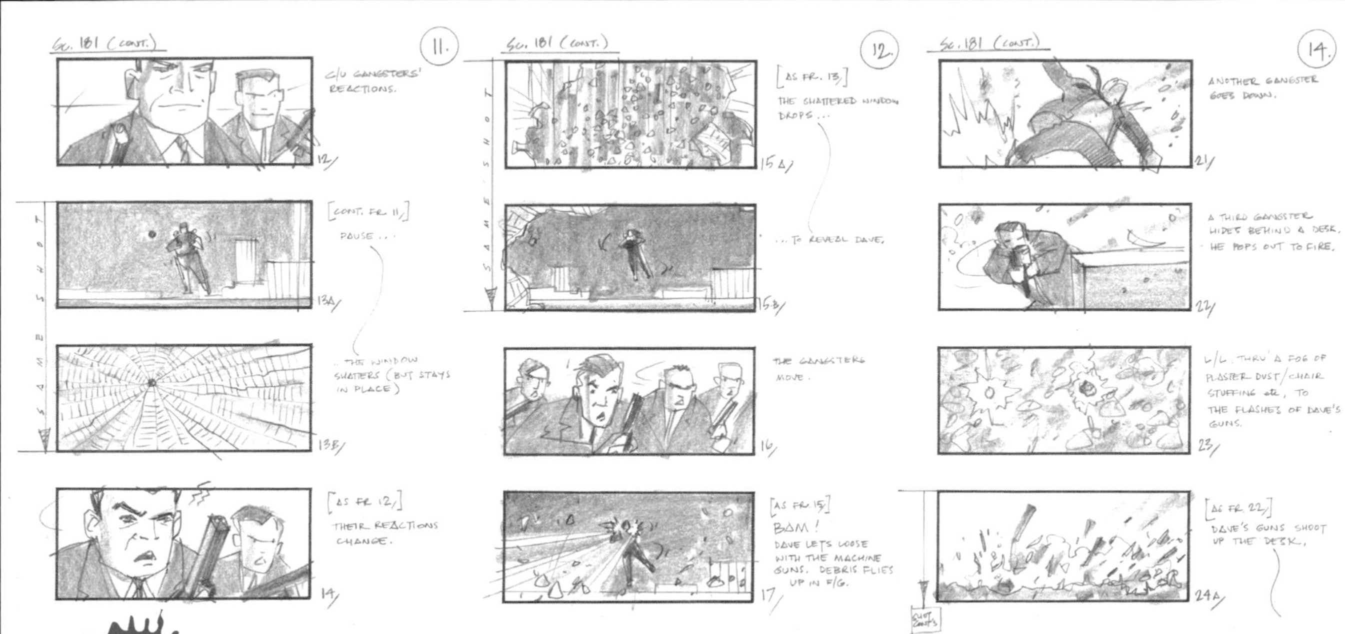

RUSSELL DE ROZARIO ON...

DESTROYING FRANK'S APARTMENT SET

We designed a massive kitchen, based on a kitchen that Matthew liked that he had seen somewhere, and we incorporated fragile elements into that, like the glass tables, so you'd be looking at that and thinking, "Christ, when's that going to explode?" Then we made a massive sofa that was supposed to look like a megalomaniac's sofa, which conveniently, because we'd made it in removable sections, we could blow the sections up and keep blowing them up until they got the shot right.

One of the things I've always really liked about my job is you go in, work really hard, make something that's really beautiful — or really ugly or really exciting or boring or whatever it is — and then smash the fucking hell out of it and sling it in a skip and it's gone. It just exists in that brief moment in time. Often people say, "Oh, it's only a film set so it's temporary anyway," but the craftsmen that build it are as good if not better than anywhere else in the world, and they build out of the same materials. People think somehow we use wood that evaporates after a few days or paint made with secret ink or whatever but it's all *real* stuff, the same timber, the same flooring. But it lives its life, a really concentrated life in a short amount of time, and it's great to get shot of it, just blow it up. So seeing it machine-gunned to pieces and bazookas going off in there is quite satisfying.

It's only a shame that that's not the way we can actually get rid of it — just torch it. I did that once — just dragged a set out to a car park and burnt it, just out of sheer spite — but I won't be allowed to do that this time. God it was great, poured petrol all over it and that was it, it went up in fifty-foot flames, licking up into the sky. It all burnt through, though it did leave a bit of a mark on the concrete...

MINDY
You are so fucking dead.
BRONZE PLATED LEGS
DETAIL: FRANK'S DESK
3X1/2 INCH METAL
BOX SECTION REBATED
INTO MDF OR PLY BOTTOM
BOX SECTION OR RODS
WELDED ON TO METAL FRAME

CHLOË MORETZ ON...

HIT-GIRL'S WEAPONS

It's great. They taught me how to load a gun, how to unload a gun, how to take it apart, how to put it back together, how to shoot one, what to do with it when it's loaded, where to keep it, and what to do with it in everyday life if you need it.

I have the Chinese stars, I have my stun grenades, smoke grenades, guns, knives, the Mindy-stick, which I love, it's my favorite, as it's just a normal stick with two humungous Gitano blades on the end. It's awesome.

I've got this really funny story: We were doing a dolly shot, I had ten blanks in the gun and I was like, boom, boom, boom, shooting directly into the camera lens. I was so scared. Then the guy on the camera went boom and the camera banana-d straight off the wall. I was shooting in his direction and I thought a bullet had come out or something so I thought, "Oh my gosh, have I just killed somebody?"

Nothing happened, he had just fallen off the dolly, but I was freaked out!

AARON JOHNSON ON...

FIGHT TRAINING

My training was: "Make sure you don't go to the gym."

"Why's that?"

"Because you've got to be skinny."

"Oh, okay!"

That's alright for me, so I didn't do much.

I think Chloë crammed three months' worth of training into the first four weeks of shooting. She's pretty ripped now for a little girl and beats us up constantly.

I have a few fight scenes where I have to learn the choreography and stuff. It's kind of nicer when it's not learnt so well, because it's a young boy waving bats about and stuff. It's not supposed to look really neat and sharp, it's very messy. You've got to believe this kid's just put on a mask and gone into a fight and is waving bats around. It's supposed to be quite natural, in the moment, instinct.

Now we have two fights going on. Mindy vs. Frank and Dave vs. Chris. The former a spectacular display of fighting prowess, the second essentially a messy scrap between two frightened kids in superhero costumes.

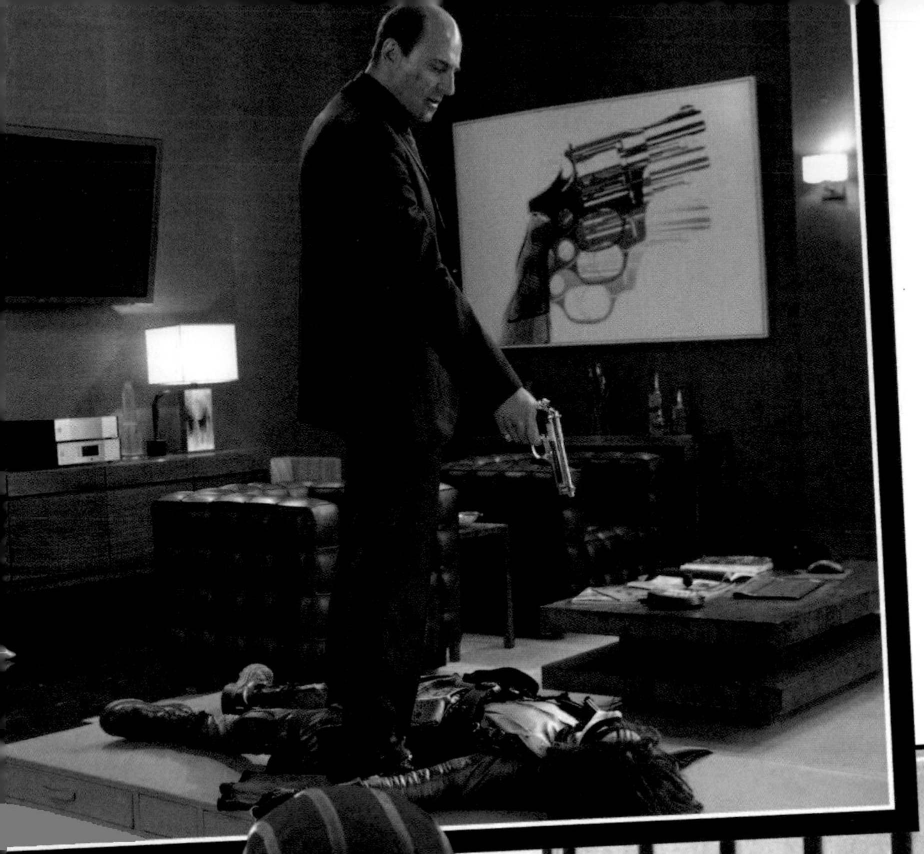

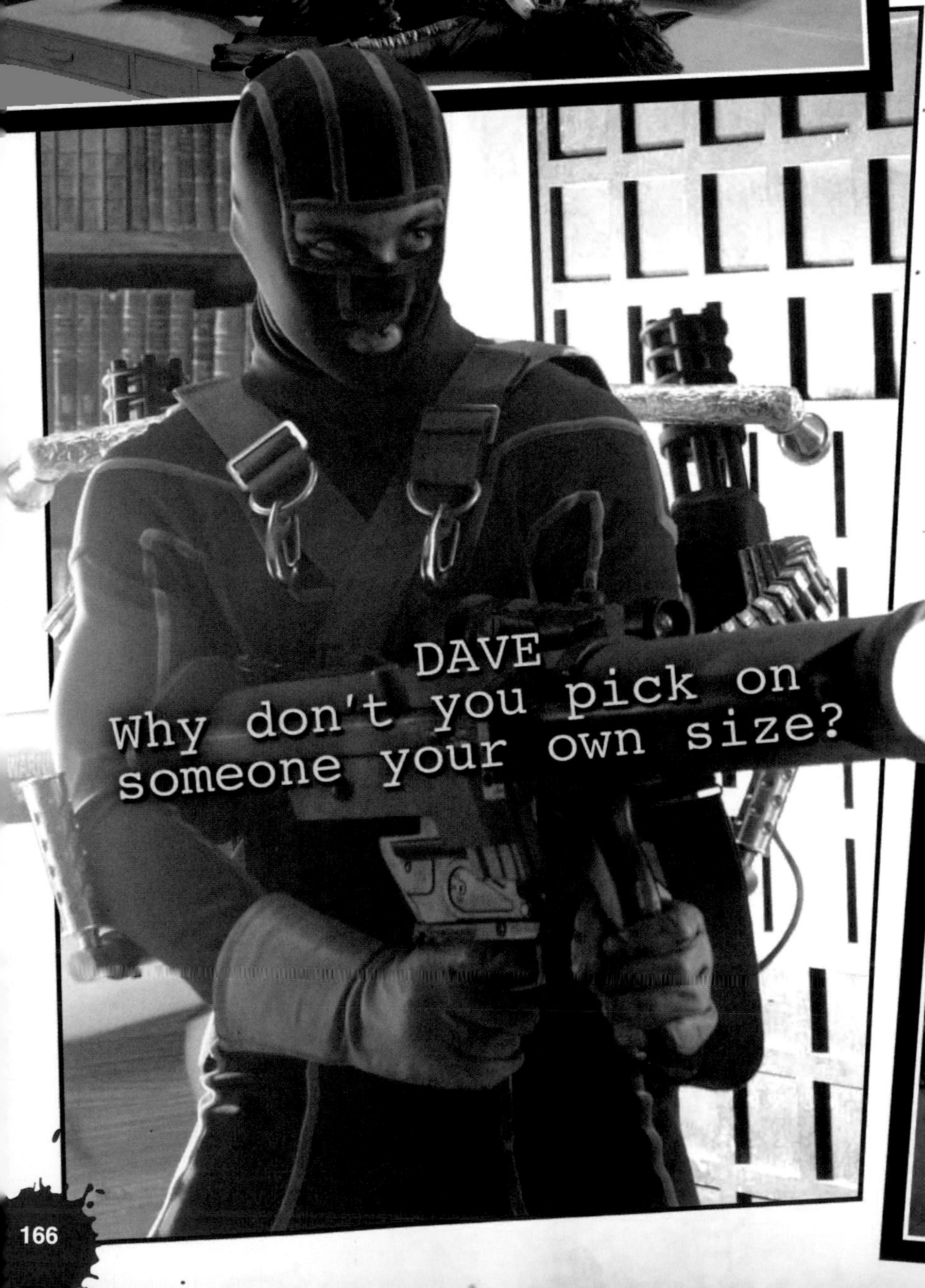

Sc. 184 (CONT.)

5.

TRACK AFTER THEM AS THEY FLY BETWEEN BUILDINGS.

PAN TO FOLLOW THEM AS THEY FLY PAST.

TRACKING BACK C/U TO SEE THEIR REACTIONS.

TIGHT C/U.

Sc. 184 (NEW YORK STREETS) + EXT. ROOFTOP - DAWN.

4

THEY FLY OVER US. CAMERA TILTS UP TO FOLLOW.

LOOKING DOWN - THEY TURN ROUND A CORNER.

THEY FLY OVER US. CAMERA FOLLOWS THEM.

TRACKING BACK WITH THEM AS THEY FLY ALONG PAST BUILDINGS.

DAVE
Why don't you pick on someone your own size?

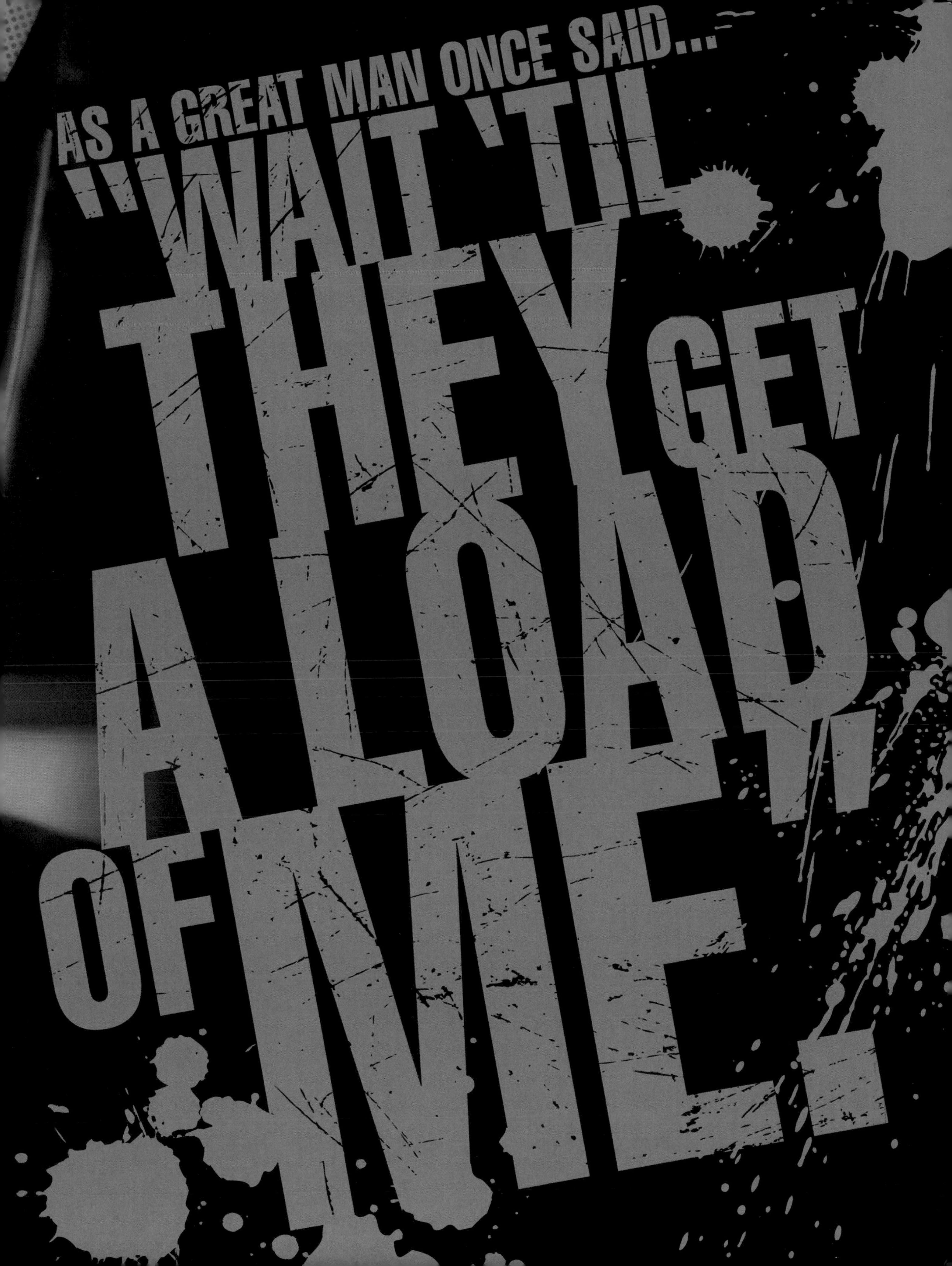
AS A GREAT MAN ONCE SAID...
"WAIT 'TIL
THEY GET
A LOAD
OF ME."

MARK MILLAR ON...

RED-MIST: SUPERVILLAIN

Red Mist surviving, becoming the supervillain was always planned, but the idea was that he was going to be a more minor character in the first film. Then we saw what Chris was capable of! Also, I really like the idea of somebody who people were relaxed watching on screen doing horrible things. In this movie he doesn't do anything *too* horrible — it's pretty bad though! — but the second movie, it's going to get very, *very* dark, what goes on with him. The analogy I always make is *Once Upon a Time in the West*, when you see Henry Fonda shoot a kid — it's so shocking. That's the thing I always remember from that film, because the audience relaxes when they see Henry Fonda, and you think, "Well, nothing too bad's going to happen," and then he shoots a kid. I love playing around with people's emotions like that. So the idea of McLovin' and the fun Red Mist doing something horrible is genuinely quite disturbing when you see it happen. We couldn't have got away with that with another actor. The minute we saw his performance, we were looking at each other and realized how good he was and what we could do with him in the future...

Opposite top: Millar's original notes for *Kick-Ass* issue 4, where he first comes up with the idea of Red Mist as supervillain.
Opposite: The invitation to the movie's wrap party.

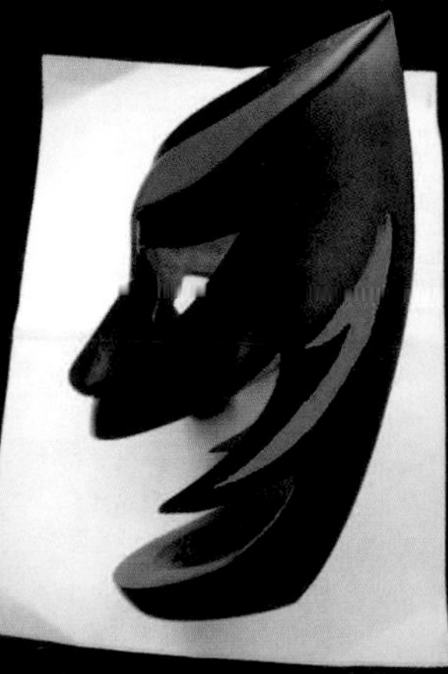

VOLUME TWO

A lot of the stuff I was going to put in Volume 1 ended up in Volume 2. One of my favorite ideas in superhero comics is the exposure of the secret identity, that being endangered. Every issue of *Superman* I ever read growing up, the cover was Superman about to have his secret identity exposed. It's really weird when you look back at all the covers. It was probably in the '60s and '70s when something like seventy per cent of the covers showed someone exposing his secret identity, but it's something that's never done now. The last ten years or so most of the identities *are* public and it's not such a big deal any more. It's quite an odd thing. So I liked the idea of doing that to somebody like Kick-Ass, who's going to have real-world ramifications if his secret identity gets exposed. I wanted that in the first volume but there was just no room, so I shifted it all into the second volume.

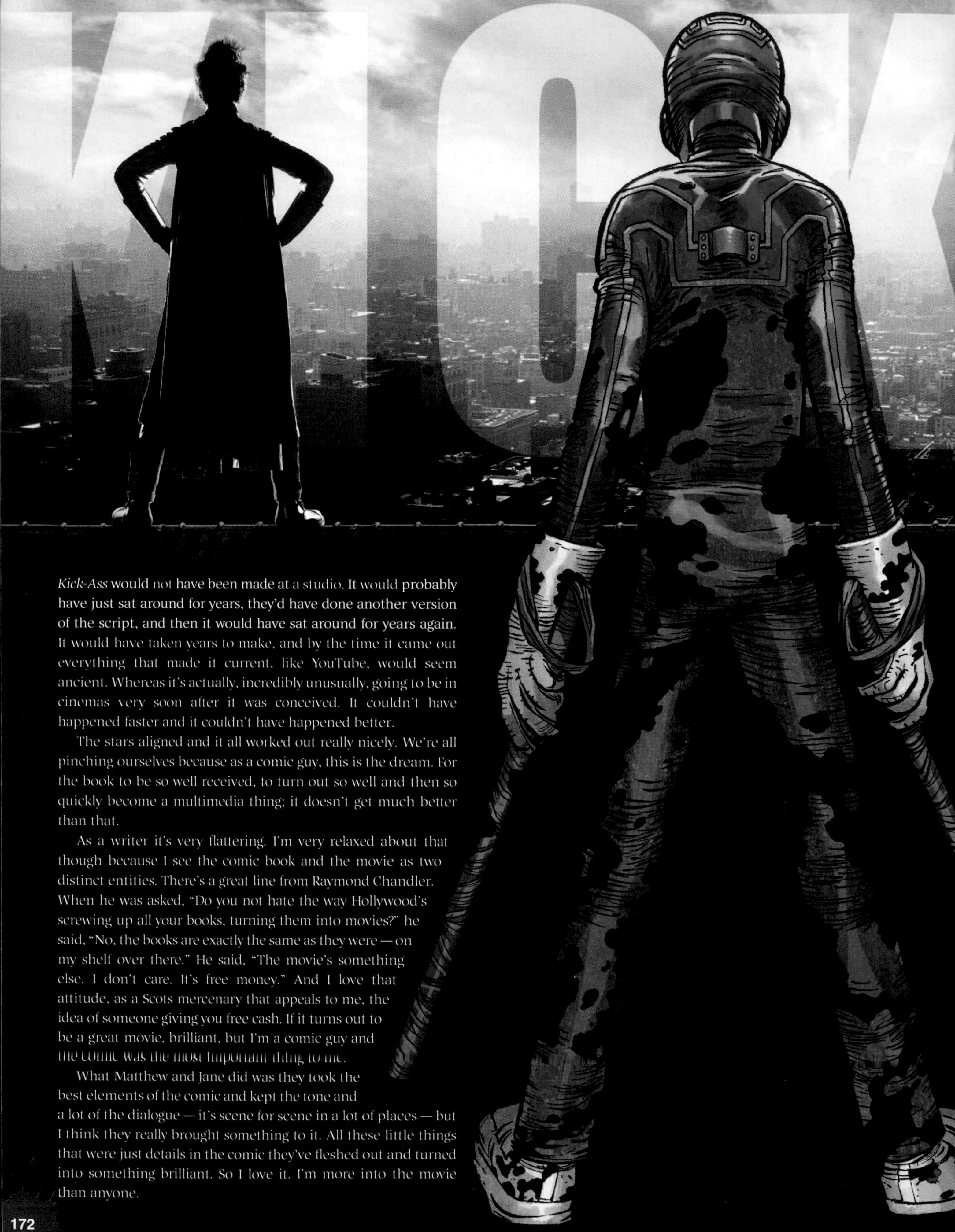

Kick-Ass would not have been made at a studio. It would probably have just sat around for years, they'd have done another version of the script, and then it would have sat around for years again. It would have taken years to make, and by the time it came out everything that made it current, like YouTube, would seem ancient. Whereas it's actually, incredibly unusually, going to be in cinemas very soon after it was conceived. It couldn't have happened faster and it couldn't have happened better.

The stars aligned and it all worked out really nicely. We're all pinching ourselves because as a comic guy, this is the dream. For the book to be so well received, to turn out so well and then so quickly become a multimedia thing; it doesn't get much better than that.

As a writer it's very flattering. I'm very relaxed about that though because I see the comic book and the movie as two distinct entities. There's a great line from Raymond Chandler. When he was asked, "Do you not hate the way Hollywood's screwing up all your books, turning them into movies?" he said, "No, the books are exactly the same as they were — on my shelf over there." He said, "The movie's something else. I don't care. It's free money." And I love that attitude, as a Scots mercenary that appeals to me, the idea of someone giving you free cash. If it turns out to be a great movie, brilliant, but I'm a comic guy and the comic was the most important thing to me.

What Matthew and Jane did was they took the best elements of the comic and kept the tone and a lot of the dialogue — it's scene for scene in a lot of places — but I think they really brought something to it. All these little things that were just details in the comic they've fleshed out and turned into something brilliant. So I love it. I'm more into the movie than anyone.

JANE GOLDMAN ON…

THE SEQUEL

Chloë feels that it would be very important for Hit Girl to have a purple motorbike, so that's the main thing we've thought about if this continues! Hit Girl will get a purple motorbike. In terms of what happens to Kick-Ass and Red Mist, there's such a rich, rich thing going on there, you kind of try and stop your mind running away with it, but it's hard not to, which is a great thing. It's very fertile ground…

Right and below: Pencils and finished art for Romita's movie poster, which debuted at San Diego Comic-Con 2009.

> I was the little guy who refused to give up. The world's first real-life superhero.

MARK MILLAR ON...

THE FRANCHISE

In book terms this is a franchise. We'll keep this running for a little while — we're going to milk this cash cow for all that it's worth! But we also have a really good time doing it. I've got this idiot attention span, I get really bored really fast and usually I don't stay on anything for more than ten or twelve issues, but I could write this for a couple of years I think. I've got a lot of ideas for it, which is really unusual for me, and I'm seeing this as a big, long-term thing.

Hopefully the movies will follow in the same fashion. Matthew seems jazzed about it all and everybody's so good working on it, so hopefully... bring on more of that free cash!

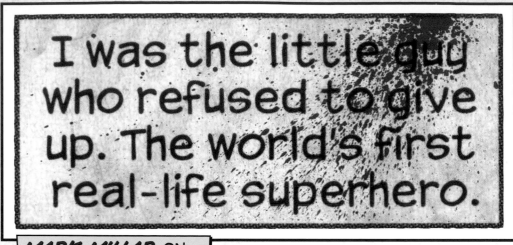

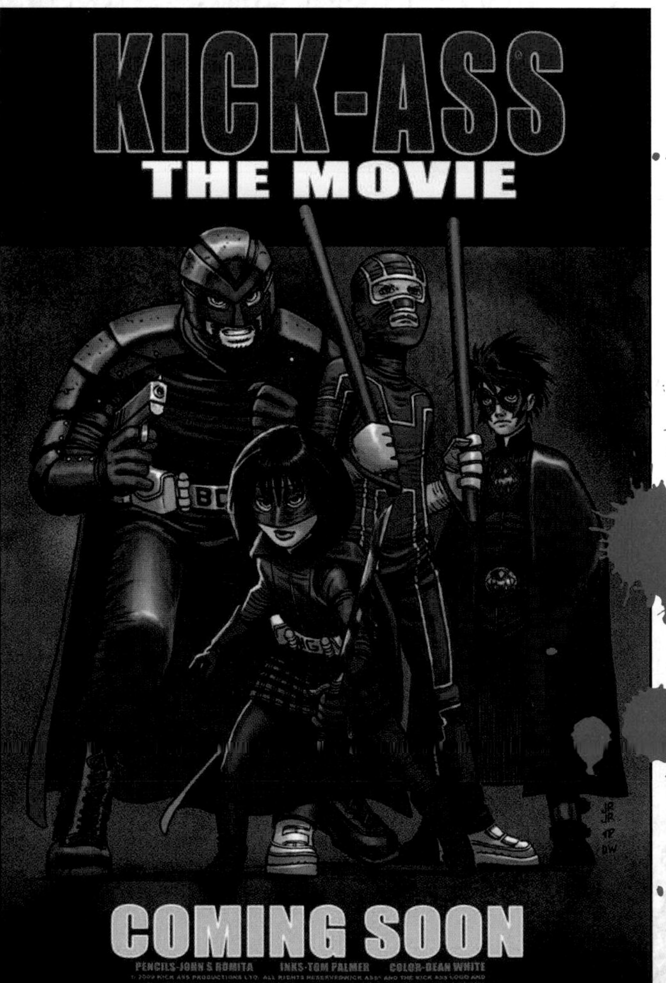

MATTHEW VAUGHN ON...

KICK-ASS 2

I don't want to tempt fate, but Mark and I, over a couple of beers, came up with the funniest, coolest idea for a sequel, that we would only be able to get away with if the film does well. We'd dial it up to eleven, shall we say...

BD
HG

I CAN'T FLY.
BUT I CAN KICK YOUR ASS.
⚠CAUTION
STAND CLEAR WHEN
CONTAINER IS
BEING LIFTED
KICK-
ASS